Contents

Preface

Development Economics rightly remains a key area of economics. This new edition of Frederick Nixson's popular book draws on recent advances in development theory, changes in the world economy and the response of international organizations to the question of development. It is designed to cover the requirements of Module 2886 of the OCR A level examination and Unit 5B of Edexcel's A level exam. It should also prove to be a valuable resource for students following university courses in Development Economics.

Frederick Nixson is an acknowledged expert in development economics. He is Professor of Development Economics at the University of Manchester, and his work in the field takes him throughout the world, giving him first-hand experience of the issues involved.

Susan Grant
Series Editor

STUDIES IN ECONOMICS AND BUSINESS

Development Economics

Second edition

Frederick Nixson

Professor of Development Economics
University of Manchester

Series Editor
Susan Grant
West Oxfordshire College

Dedicated to Alexandra

Heinemann Educational Publishers
Halley Court, Jordan Hill, Oxford OX2 8EJ
a division of Reed Educational & Professional Publishing Ltd

OXFORD MELBOURNE AUCKLAND
JOHANNESBURG BLANTYRE GABORONE
IBADAN PORTSMOUTH (NH) USA CHICAGO

Heinemann is a registered trademark of Reed Educational & Professional Publishing Ltd

First published in 2001

05 04 03 02 01
10 9 8 7 6 5 4 3 2

British Library Cataloguing in Publication Data
A catalogue record for this book is available from the British Library

ISBN 0 435 330489

Typeset and Illustrated by TechType
Printed and bound by Biddles Ltd

338·9 NIX

R13688

Acknowledgements
The publishers would like to thank the following for permission to reproduce copyright material:
Cambridge University Press and author Peter Townsend for the excerpt on p.55; the Department for International Development (DFID) for the bar chart on p.6; © The Economist Newspaper Ltd, London for the article and data on pp.15–17, the article on pp.108–9, and the article and graph on pp.52–4; Edexcel Foundation for the questions on pp.26, 52–4, 61–3, 72–3, 98–9, 108–9; *The Guardian* for articles on pp.8, 67, 106; *Human Development Report 1998* by the United Nations Development Program (UNDP) © 1998 by the UNDP, used by permission of Oxford University Press (OUP) Inc for the table data on p.26 (see also *World Development Report 1998* below); The OCR for questions on pp. 38–40, 61, 83, 98, 108, 118–19, (reproduced with the kind permission of the OCR); the OECD for data on pp. 111, 112, 113 (from *Development Co-operation Report 1998: Efforts and Policies of the Members of the Development Assistance Committee*, 1999 edition, © OECD 1999); ODI and authors Lucia Hanmer and Felix Naschold for the data on p.9, ODI for the data on p.88; Sage Publications and author Peter Dicken for the diagram on p.42 and the table on p.96, both of which appeared on pp.36 and 60 of *Global Shift*, 1998; UCLES for questions on pp.11, 25, 83, 84–5, 38, 118 (Reproduced by permission of the University of Cambridge Local Examinations Syndicate.); the UN for the table on p.101, the UNCTAD for the use of tables on pp.87, 92, 102, 103, 104; the UNDP for tables on pp.18, 19, 20 and for the graph on p.56; UNIDO for the table on p.79; the World Bank for the material on pp.22–3, 40, 58, 66, 78; *World Development Report 1998* by World Bank © 1998 by the International Bank for Reconstruction and Development (IBRD) /World Bank, used by permission of Oxford University Press OUP Inc. for the table data on p.26 (see also *Human Development Report 1998*, above); World Development Report 1990 by World Bank © 1990 by the IBRD/World Bank, used by permission of OUP Inc. for the table data on p.62; *World Development Report 1994* by World Bank © 1994 by the IBRD/World Bank, used by permission of OUP Inc. for the table data on p. 72–3.

The publishers have made every effort to contact copyright holders. However, if any material has been incorrectly acknowledged, the publishers would be pleased to correct this at the earliest opportunity.

Tel: 01865 888058 www.heinemann.co.uk

ii

Introduction

Developing countries cover more than two-thirds of the Earth's land surface and they account for more than four-fifths of the world's population. Over 150 countries are variously classified as low- or middle-income, newly industrializing or petroleum exporting, and they vary greatly in size, structure, level of development – especially with respect to their level of industrialization, history and culture.

To attempt to capture and explain this diversity in a short book is ambitious. But development economists believe that common elements can be found and useful generalizations made. The economist provides one part of the explanation of poverty, growth and development, using ideas and concepts drawn from orthodox economic analysis and new concepts and techniques drawn from the study of poor countries themselves. Other social scientists – sociologists, political scientists, geographers – help to complete the explanation.

This book is thus an introduction to a huge subject – the study of economic development.

This second edition maintains the basic structure of the first edition and revises and updates as necessary. A number of new issues are introduced: pro-poor growth and poverty alleviation (Chapter 1); the Lewis model and vicious circles (Chapter 3); globalization and the 1997 Asian financial crisis (Chapter 4); the World Trade Organization (Chapter 8); and the highly indebted poor countries (Chapter 10).

- Chapter 1 gives an overview of the dimensions of *global poverty* and considers the different ways by which poverty can be measured.
- Chapter 2 discusses the notion of *development*, distinguishing it from *economic growth*; highlights problems of measurement; and outlines the *human development index* as an example of a *composite indicator* of development.
- Chapter 3 surveys *development theory*. The original theoretical contributions of development economists are noted and alternative theoretical perspectives discussed.
- Chapter 4 places the discussion of development within the broader *global context*. Developing countries in the 1980s were subject to a series of unprecedented *external shocks* from which many of them have found it difficult to recover. The 1997 Asian financial crisis was a further shock to the global economy.
- Chapter 5 returns to a central concern of development – the

1

distribution of income in poor countries. The possible link between more rapid economic growth and greater income inequality is noted, but it is emphasized that there is no single economic model linking growth and equity.

- Chapter 6 is concerned with *population* and *the environment*. Both topics are important in their own right but they are linked closely together in the development process.
- Chapter 7 focuses on *agricultural* and *industrial development* and highlights the rise of the *newly industrializing countries* (NICs). The latter return us to the question of different theoretical perspectives and this highlights conflicting notions of the role of the state in the development process.
- Chapter 8 considers *international trade* in more detail, with particular attention focused on the *terms of trade* of poor, primary commodity exporting countries.
- Chapter 9 discusses the role of *transnational corporations* (TNCs) in development, and some conflicts of interest between TNCs and host countries are noted.
- Chapter 10 concludes the book with a discussion of the issues relating to *aid* and *debt*. The complexity of both the *aid relationship* and the *debt crisis* is emphasized, and the changing roles of the *World Bank* and *International Monetary Fund* are noted.

A note on terminology

The poor countries of the world are referred to by a variety of terms – underdeveloped, less developed, developing, the Third World, the South.

The developed market (capitalist) economies – the 'First World' – are seen as forming the core of the global economy. The poor countries – the 'Third World' – constitute a dependent periphery.

The former 'Second World' – the centrally planned command economies of eastern and central Europe and the former Soviet Union (FSU) – are now referred to as 'transitional economies', in the process of moving from a planned to a free market economy.

Some poorer economies which once had socialist development objectives – Tanzania, Mozambique, Laos, Mongolia, for example – have abandoned those objectives and have implemented economic and political reforms. Others, such as China and Vietnam, have not formally abandoned their socialist development objectives, but have implemented massive reform programmes such that the market mechanism, and not the plan, is the main allocator of resources.

Two socialist economies – Cuba and North Korea – continue to resist change. Elsewhere we see the emergence of the NICs – South Korea, Taiwan, Singapore and Hong Kong, China (the original 'Gang of Four'), and Malaysia Thailand and Indonesia. At the other end of the income spectrum, the United Nations' Conference on Trade and Development (UNCTAD) categorizes 48 of the poorest countries as 'least developed'.

Use of all the above terminology gives rise to problems.

- If we refer to poor countries as 'less' or 'under' or 'least' developed, we must pose the question – with respect to what? Implicitly we are comparing these economies and their levels of development to the developed market economies and the latter thus become a 'model' for poor countries to copy. This may not be appropriate, however, given that poor countries may wish to pursue development objectives that are different from those represented by developed market economies (although this is less likely since the disappearance of the 'Second World' and the model of development that it represented).
- More importantly, it may not be possible to replicate the experience of the developed market economy. We can draw lessons from the experience of other countries (although history does not repeat itself) and each country must define its own path to development.
- The notion of a 'Third World' is also misleading. It implies a separateness from the 'First World' which does not in fact exist. Poor countries are linked in a variety of ways to the developed market economies – through trade, financial flows, and cultural and military links ('globalization') – and thus development and growth in poor countries is in part determined by decisions taken in developed economies and in global institutions.

Terminology is thus important because it colours the way that we consider problems of global poverty and inequality and formulate policies for their alleviation.

Suggested reading
- Annual reports

The World Bank publishes both an *Annual Report* (free) and the annual *World Development Report*, published by Oxford University Press for the World Bank. It has been published annually since 1978 and each year now has a theme (Poverty, Environment, Employment, etc.). The United Nations' Conference on Trade and Development

(UNCTAD) publishes an annual *Trade and Development* report and *The Least Developed Countries Report*. *Finance and Development* is the quarterly publication of the IMF and the World Bank (free). The European Union (EU) publishes *The Courier* (free), containing a wealth of material on the ACP (African, Pacific and Caribbean) countries. The United Nations' Development Programme (UNDP) publishes an annual *Human Development Report* (Oxford University Press for the UN).

● Aid statistics

Aid statistics are to be found in the OECD's annual *Development Co-operation Report* (OECD, Paris).

● Other publications

Oxfam has published *The Oxfam Poverty Report* (1995), which is a good indication of the non-governmental organization view of development. The Overseas Development Institute (ODI) in London publishes a series of invaluable *Briefing Papers*. *The Economist* and *The Financial Times* publish many articles dealing with Third World issues, especially on commodities, international business and finance.

Chapter One

Poverty: the global dimensions

'What is vital for the health of our global society today is that governments and citizens set their forces towards global poverty eradication.' Oxfam, 1995

It has been estimated that, in 1990 (the base year from which calculations are made), 1.3 billion people were living in absolute **poverty** in the developing world. This was about one-quarter of the world's population or 30 per cent of the total number of people living in developing countries.

To make this definition of poverty useful, three questions must be answered:

- How do we measure the **standard of living**?
- What is meant by a minimal standard of living?
- Having identified the poor, how can the extent of poverty be expressed in a single measure or index?

Measuring the standard of living

Household incomes and expenditures *per capita* are most commonly used to provide a quantitatively defined standard of poverty and to make comparisons between countries or regions. Such measures do not, however, include such aspects of **welfare** as health, life expectancy, literacy and access to key goods such as clean drinking water. Because of these weaknesses, *consumption-based poverty measures* are used as a measure of well-being.

The poverty line

All measures of poverty relate to a given norm or average, and the consumption-based **poverty line** comprises two elements:

- The expenditure necessary to buy a minimum standard of nutrition and other basic necessities, and
- *'a further amount that varies from country to country, reflecting the cost of participating in the everyday life of society'* (World Bank).

The first element can be calculated in a straightforward manner. The cost of minimum adequate caloric intakes and other necessities is estimated from the prices of the goods that constitute the consumption bundles of the poor. The second element, however, is subjective and varies with *per capita* income – that is, the *richer* a country is, the *higher* is its poverty line.

Poverty can thus be viewed as either an *absolute* or a *relative* concept. *Absolute* poverty is defined as people living below a 'poverty line' of US$1 per day, measured in terms of *per capita* consumption (which is less variable than income) at 1993 purchasing power parity prices (PPP – see Chapter 2 for an explanation). At this level of *per capita* income, people are not able to attain a minimal standard of living (according to the World Bank). Poverty as a relative concept is discussed in Chapter 5.

How much poverty is there?

Using the *headcount method* gives us the above-quoted estimate of 1.3 billion poor people in developing countries in poverty in 1990. Figure 1 illustrates the regional distribution of people living in poverty. Extremely poor people are concentrated in certain regions:

- South Asia: 40 per cent of the population live in extreme poverty, accounting for 43 per cent of the global total of poor people in 1996.
- Sub-Saharan Africa: 48 per cent of the population live in extreme poverty, accounting for 24 per cent of the global total.

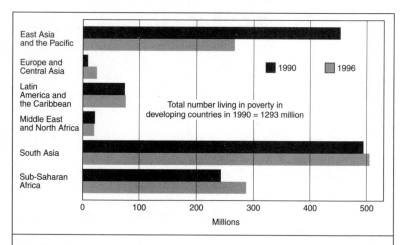

Figure 1 Populations living on incomes of less than $1 (PPP) a day (millions)

Source: DFID, *Halving world poverty by 2015: economic growth and security,* consultation document, September 2000

• East Asia: 15 per cent of the population live in extreme poverty, accounting for 22 per cent of the global total (note that this figure was estimated before the 1997 East Asian financial crisis which has raised the incidence of poverty in several of the affected economies).

Given the large numbers of poor people that live in India and China, the reduction of poverty in these two countries will have a significant effect on the global total. Economic growth in China continues to be translated into poverty reduction, in part reflecting the Chinese government's emphasis on job creation, the provision of rural health facilities, effective distribution of food to both cities and countryside, and a general guarantee of social security (note, however, that these conditions may be changing as China liberalizes and opens up its economy to market forces). The Indian situation gives more cause for concern as the data indicate that the more rapid growth experienced in the 1990s has had only a limited impact on the incidence of poverty.

Poverty is usually worse in rural than in urban areas, as is malnutrition, lack of education and poor housing. The extent of poverty varies among rural areas, however, with the poor located in regions where arable land tends to be scarce, agricultural productivity is low, and drought, floods and environmental degradation are common.

In urban areas the poor typically live in slums or squatter settlements and suffer from overcrowding, poor or non-existent sanitation facilities, and contaminated water supplies. Poor households tend to be large, although it is not clear whether households are poor because they are large or large because they are poor (that is, it is essential to have large numbers of children to ensure that some survive to support the household when parents are old). Either way, poor children are vulnerable to disease and malnutrition, and poverty-related illnesses can cause permanent damage. Women, too, are disproportionately represented among the poor and are severely disadvantaged with respect to health, nutrition, education and employment.

Eradication of poverty: global cooperation and national commitment

The international community and bilateral agencies (for example the UK Department for International Development – DFID) have adopted a number of international development goals, including the target of reducing by a half the proportion of people living in absolute poverty by the year 2015 – that is, to reduce the proportion of the extremely poor to 12.5 per cent of the global population. Global population is expected to grow over this period to about 7.3 billion people, and so to reach the poverty alleviation target about a billion people will need to be lifted above the poverty line.

Even if this target is reached, however, there will still be 0.9 billion people living in absolute poverty, so the problem will have by no means disappeared.

The rates of economic growth needed to achieve the global poverty alleviation target are given in Table 1 along with historical rates of growth of GDP *per capita*. It can be seen from the table that only the region of East Asia and the Pacific has achieved historical rates of

Poverty reduction hopes hit despite better growth

MARK ATKINSON

The World Bank yesterday upgraded its global growth forecasts but said international targets for poverty reduction are likely to be missed as developing countries continued to suffer from the after-shock of the Asian crisis.

The bank says in an update of its March predictions that output in the Group of Seven industrialised countries will expand by 2.6% this year, 0.9 percentage points higher than projected six months ago. The change is largely due to the unexpected strength of the US economy and the quicker than anticipated upswing in Japan.

With economic activity in the east Asian countries, especially Korea, rebounding, developing countries as a whole will enjoy faster growth, with output growing by 2.7% instead of 1.5%, says the bank in its annual Global Economic Prospects and the Developing Countries report.

However, these upward revisions mask a "fragile and uneven" performance by developing countries, many of which are struggling to recover from the financial crisis of 1997/98. Long-term growth prospects are worse than before it struck.

Excluding Russia and eastern Europe, growth in developing countries is projected to average 5% a year in 2002–2008, a much faster rate than in industrial countries, but significantly lower than the pre-crisis 1990s ...

The bank concludes that the internationally agreed goal of halving world poverty by 2015 is unlikely to be reached. East and south Asia should cut poverty by half or more, eastern Europe, central Asia, the Middle East and north Africa should see a significant reduction, but sub-Saharan Africa and Latin America are likely to experience a rise in poverty.

The Guardian, 8 December 1999

Table 1 Growth rates required (in GDP *per capita*) to halve proportion of poor by 2015

Region	Growth required (2000–15)	Historical growth (1965–97)	(1990–97)
Sub-Saharan Africa	5.9	–0.2	–0.7
Middle East and North Africa	2.8	0.1	0.7
East Asia and Pacific	3.5	5.4	7.7
South Asia	3.9	2.3	3.3
Latin America and Caribbean	7.0	1.3	2.1
Eastern Europe and Central Asia	3.8	3.2	–4.1

Source: Lucia Hanmer and Felix Nasehold, 'Attaining the International Development Targets: will growth be enough', *Development Policy Review*, March 2000, vol. 18, issue 1

growth above the growth rate required to achieve the poverty alleviation target. South Asia has seen some acceleration of economic growth over the period 1990–97, but it is still below the required target rate of growth.

For sub-Saharan Africa, with negative rates of growth of GDP *per capita* over the 1965–97 period, and to a lesser extent Latin America and the Caribbean, where at least growth rates have been positive, the target for poverty alleviation looks very difficult, if not impossible to achieve.

DFID notes that there are three fundamental requirements for reaching the poverty alleviation targets.

- Economic growth is a necessary but not sufficient condition.
- Economic growth must take into account equity considerations; that is, it must be pro-poor (see the boxed item 'What is pro-poor growth?' on page 10).
- The vulnerability of the poor to shocks (conflicts, bad weather, economic fluctuations) needs to be reduced.

The alleviation of poverty is of course an important aim of development (perhaps *the* most important – see Chapter 2). No one doubts the urgency of the need to alleviate, and ultimately eliminate, global poverty. But rhetoric is not always matched by action, so deep divisions of opinion remain as to how problems of poverty can best be tackled.

What is pro-poor growth?

There are various ways of defining **pro-poor growth**, but it is generally identified as being 'broad-based' and labour-intensive. It needs to:

- create jobs for the unemployed and underemployed
- improve the productivity of those in work and/or those who are time-constrained – women for example
- recognize that different strategies are required for the rural landless, smallholders and workers in the informal sector.

DFID argues that economic growth must '... include the poor by maximising their opportunities and by utilising their skills, time and physical resources. Poor people require improved access to health, education, markets and assets. Through this, they will be enabled to contribute to economic growth and benefit from increased national income.'

On the one hand, there are those countries and institutions (the USA and the World Bank, for example) that argue for pro-market policies, emphasizing the liberalization of the economy and minimal state intervention. Emphasis is placed on agricultural development, employment creation through the use of labour-intensive technologies, and investment in health and education to raise the quality of human capital (**human resource development**).

While not denying the importance of such policies, other institutions, including the UN family and development-related institutions, and more radical political leaders, emphasize the importance of global factors which trap poor countries in a poverty cycle and make their escape from poverty difficult, if not impossible. Low commodity prices, poor trading opportunities, already inadequate and falling real values of official development assistance (aid), and the debt crisis all point to the need to transform the global economy and its institutions in order to give **Third World** countries, now often referred to as developing countries, a better deal.

It is difficult to see how the poverty alleviation target can be achieved without greater international efforts (more and better aid, debt relief) and a national commitment to economic growth which will lead directly to the reduction in poverty (more equitable income distribution, the creation of more jobs). Such actions will require changes in attitudes and policies, both globally and nationally, which have not always been forthcoming in the past.

> ### KEY WORDS
>
> | Poverty | Pro-poor growth |
> |---|---|
> | Standard of living | Human resource development |
> | Welfare | Third World |
> | Poverty line | |

Further reading

Anderton, A., Unit 99 in *Economics*, 3rd edn, Causeway Press, 2000.

Beardshaw, J. *et al.*, Chapter 46 in *Economics: A Student's Guide*, 4th edn, Longman, 1998.

Grant, S., and Vidler, C., A2 Section 5 Unit 24 in *Economics in Context*, Heinemann, 2000.

Griffiths, A., and Wall, S. (eds), Chapter 30 in *Applied Economics*, 8th edn, Longman, 1999.

Useful websites

List of economic development sites: www.oneworld.org/partners/index.html

Department for International Development: www.dfid.gov.uk

International Labour Office: www.ilo.org

Essay topics

1. (a) Why have some countries been able to grow more rapidly than others? [8 marks]

   (b) Discuss the costs and benefits of achieving economic development. [12 marks]

   [UCLES, March 1997]

2. (a) Distinguish between absolute and relative poverty. [6 marks]

   (b) Discuss the aims which the UK government and international institutions have set for world poverty reduction. [6 marks]

   (c) Assess the requirements needed to reduce poverty. [8 marks]

Chapter Two

The meaning and measurement of economic development

'*Development means modernization, and modernization means transformation of human beings. Development as an objective and development as a process both embrace a change in fundamental attitudes to life and work, and in social, cultural and political institutions.*'   Paul Streeten, distinguished development economist and chairman of the Board of World Development

The development process is *multidimensional*. That is, it involves changes over time not only in the economy but also in institutions, political and social structures and cultural values.

Development implies *progress or improvement*, which in turn means that we make **value judgements** as to what is deemed desirable or undesirable.

Development is thus a *normative* concept and the definition of development will vary between individuals, political parties and countries. My definition of development may differ from that of others and I may feel that my definition is superior. I cannot prove that superiority, however, I can only assert it – my definition of development is merely different from, not better than, yours.

If we accept that the notion of **economic development** embodies value judgements, it is clear that *economic growth and economic development are not synonymous*. GDP *per capita* might be rising, but at the same time poverty might be increasing, inequality in the distribution of income might be rising and massive environmental damage might be occurring. It would be difficult to describe such a situation as progress! Economic growth might well be a *necessary condition* for economic development but it is not a *sufficient condition*.

The idea that economic growth need not lead to economic development led to a search for a definition of economic development. It was the British economist, Dudley Seers, who posed the question:

'*What are the necessary conditions for a universally accepted aim, the realisation of the potential of human personality?*'

Seers argued that if economic growth did *not* lead to a reduction in poverty, inequality and unemployment, then economic development

DEFINITIONS OF DEVELOPMENT

Michael Todaro argues that three basic core values should serve as a conceptual basis and practical guideline for understanding the 'inner meaning' of development. The core values are:

- sustenance: the ability to meet basic needs (food, health, shelter and protection);
- self-esteem: a sense of worth and self-respect (implying dignity, honour, recognition);
- freedom: an expanded range of choices for societies (including freedom from oppression, material wants, greater protection from environmental disasters).

Another notion of development is **sustainable development**. This is defined as 'development that meets the needs of the present without compromising the ability of future generations to meet their own needs' (World Commission on Environment and Development, 1987). A key element of this notion lies in its emphasis on maintaining **intergenerational welfare** over time – to quote the leading environmental economist, David Pearce, this involves 'providing a bequest to the next generation of an amount and quality of wealth which is at least equal to that inherited by the current generation', with wealth defined to include both the human-made and natural stock of assets. These conceptions of development raise enormous political and social issues.

- Are any countries developed on the basis of Todaro's criteria (they may be rich but that is not the same as developed)?
- Are current models of development sustainable, given the depletion of the Earth's natural wealth and the environmental problems (the depletion of the ozone layer, the destruction of rain forests) that are receiving increasing attention?
- Economics alone cannot provide answers to these questions.

could not be said to be occurring. Development is also increasingly seen to require political democracy and participation, issues which come under the heading of 'good governance' (see the boxed item 'Definitions of development').

The measurement of per capita income

All countries have adopted the conventions (the United Nations' Standard National Accounts) for the calculation of **gross national product** (GNP) and **gross domestic product** (GDP), and GNP or GDP *per capita* is the commonest indicator of the level of development.

'Economic growth' refers to an increase in either of these indicators. There are, however, well-known problems associated with the calculation of national income in poor countries and its use as an indicator of development:

- The necessary data are often incomplete, unreliable or not available.
- The accounting conventions are not necessarily appropriate; the services of women working in the household are excluded from national income statistics, yet in many poor countries, especially in sub-Saharan Africa, women are often responsible for running the family farm as well as working in the household.
- In most poor countries there is a large subsistence sector – that is, farmers may well consume all or a large proportion of what they produce, rather than sending it to market where it would be counted for the purposes of calculating national income. Statisticians make an allowance for this non-marketed component of output, and for rural capital formation that may not enter the national accounts – housebuilding, irrigation ditches – but it is generally accepted that the value of these activities is underestimated, thus biasing downwards the national income figures for poor countries.
- Income may be overstated for developed economies because a number of items that are included as income might better be seen as costs and hence excluded from income – the cost of travelling to work, for example, or the cost of heating the home in temperate climates.
- **Per capita income** tells us nothing about the *distribution of income*. Two countries with similar *per capita* incomes (average income per person) may have very different income distributions, with important implications for the welfare of their populations and the nature and characteristics of the development process. We look at this issue in greater detail in Chapter 5.

Significant problems arise when international comparisons of income levels are made. Income data measured in national currencies have to be converted into a common currency, usually the US dollar, and an exchange rate must thus be chosen. If poor countries artificially maintain overvalued exchange rates (that is, the price of foreign currencies in terms of their domestic currency is too low), this will overstate the income of the country expressed in US dollars.

Offsetting this, however, is the fact that many goods and services in poor countries are not traded and hence have no impact on the exchange rate. Many of the necessities of life in poor countries – basic

foodstuffs for example – are very low-priced in dollar terms, and a haircut in Kampala, Uganda, will cost less than one in Paris or London.
According to World Bank data:

- Mozambique was the poorest country in the world in 1997, with an estimated GNP *per capita* of US$90;
- Switzerland was the richest, with a GNP *per capita* of US$44 320.

Is the average Swiss citizen 500 times better off than the average Mozambican? To put that question slightly differently, does it make sense to state that in Mozambique, on average, people live on 25 cents a day?

Clearly nobody in a developed economy could survive on such a low income. Given that the majority of Mozambicans do survive, it must be the case that the necessities essential for survival cost less in Mozambique than for example in Switzerland, and/or $90 is not a meaningful estimate of *per capita* income in Mozambique. This is not to deny that a huge gap exists between the average incomes of very rich and very poor countries, nor should it lessen our concern with such inequalities. But it does mean that the gap on average is not as great as these statistics would suggest and a number of attempts have been made to compute more meaningful comparisons.

Purchasing power parity comparisons

In order to overcome the problems associated with the use of existing exchange rates, attempts have been made to compare *per capita* incomes of different countries directly by the use of 'international prices'. The theory of **purchasing power parity** (PPP) holds that, in the long run, the exchange rate of two currencies should move towards the rate that would equalize the prices of an identical basket of goods and services in each country. The boxed item on page 16 gives an example based on the price of a McDonald's Big Mac in a number of countries.

Big Mac Currencies

It is that time of the year when The Economist munches its way around the globe in order to update our Big Mac index. We first launched this 14 years ago as a light-hearted guide to whether currencies are at their 'correct' exchange rate. It is not intended as a precise predictor of exchange rates, but a tool to make economic theory more digestible.

Burgernomics is based on the theory of purchasing-power parity, the notion that a dollar should buy the same amount in all countries. Thus in the long run, the exchange rate between two currencies should move

---

The golden-arches standard

	Big Mac prices		Implied PPP* of the dollar	Actual $ exchange rate 25/04/00	Under(−)/ over(+) valuation against the dollar, %
	in local currency	in dollars			
United States†	$2.51	2.51	−	−	−
Argentina	Peso 2.50	2.50	1.00	1.00	0
Australia	A$2.59	1.54	1.03	1.68	−38
Brazil	Real 2.95	1.65	1.18	1.79	−34
Britain	1.90	3.00	1.32‡	1.58‡	+20
Canada	C$2.85	1.94	1.14	1.47	−23
Chile	Peso 1,260	2.45	502	514	−2
China	Yuan 9.90	1.20	3.94	8.28	−52
Czech Rep	Koruna 54.37	1.39	21.7	39.1	−45
Denmark	DKr 24.75	3.08	9.86	8.04	+23
Euro area	2.56	2.37	0.98§	0.93§	−5
France	FFr 18.50	2.62	7.37	7.07	+4
Germany	DM 4.99	2.37	1.99	2.11	−6
Italy	Lire 4,500	2.16	1,793	2,088	−14
Spain	Pta 375	2.09	149	179	−17
Hong Kong	HK$10.20	1.31	4.06	7.79	−48
Hungary	Forint 339	1.21	135	279	−52
Indonesia	Rupiah 14,500	1.83	5,777	7,945	−27
Israel	Shekel 14.5	3.58	5.78	4.05	+43
Japan	¥294	2.78	117	106	+11
Malaysia	M$4.52	1.19	1.80	3.80	−53
Mexico	Peso 20.90	2.22	8.33	9.41	−11
New Zealand	NZ$3.40	1.69	1.35	2.01	−33
Poland	Zloty 5.50	1.28	2.19	4.30	−49
Russia	Rouble 39.50	1.39	15.7	28.5	−45
Singapore	S$3.20	1.88	1.27	1.70	−25
South Africa	Rand 9.00	1.34	3.59	6.72	−47
South Korea	Won 3,000	2.71	1,195	1,108	+8
Sweden	SKr 24.00	2.71	9.56	8.84	+8
Switzerland	SF 5.90	3.48	2.35	1.70	+39
Taiwan	NT$70.00	2.29	27.9	30.6	−9
Thailand	Baht 55.00	1.45	21.9	38.0	−42

*Purchasing-power parity: local price divided by price in United States
†Average of New York, Chicago, San Francisco and Atlanta
‡Dollars per pound
§Dollars per euro

towards the rate that equalises the prices of an identical basket of goods and services in each country. Our 'basket' is a McDonald's Big Mac, which is produced in about 120 countries. The Big Mac PPP is the exchange rate that would mean hamburgers cost the same in America as abroad. Comparing actual exchange rates with PPPS indicates whether a currency is under or overvalued.

The first column of the table shows local-currency prices of a Big Mac; the second converts them into dollars. The average price of a Big Mac (including tax) in four American cities is $2.51. The cheapest burger among the countries in the table is once again in Malaysia ($1.19); at the other extreme the most expensive is $3.58 in Israel. This is another way of saying that the Malaysian ringgit is the most undervalued currency (by 53%), and the Israeli shekel the most overvalued (by 43%).

The third column calculates Big Mac PPPS. For instance, dividing the Japanese price by the American one gives a dollar PPP of ¥117. On April 25th the actual rate was ¥106, implying that the yen is 11% overvalued against the dollar.

Sources: McDonald's and *The Economist*, 29 April 2000

An index of human development

The most ambitious attempt to measure development is the **Human Development Index** (HDI). Human development is thus defined as enlarging people's choices. Such choices are, in principle, infinite and change over time; but at all levels of development the three essential ones are:

- for people to live a long and healthy life;
- for them to acquire knowledge;
- for them to have access to resources needed for a decent standard of living.

The HDI is a composite indicator (see the boxed item on page 18). The HDI has been adjusted by the United Nations' Development Programme (UNDP) to take into account income distribution and gender inequalities and it can be disaggregated to take into account racial inequalities (South Africa) and regional disparities within countries (Brazil, Nigeria and Egypt, for example).

The HDI ranges between 0 and 1. Table 2 gives the HDI and the GDP rankings for a sample of rich and poor countries, classified by their level of human development. It can be seen that Canada has the highest HDI value but not the highest real GDP (at PPP$) *per capita*. At the other end of the scale, Sierra Leone, the poorest country in the world (as measured by real GDP *per capita* at PPP$) also has the lowest HDI.

Why do we need a human development index?

Because national progress tends otherwise to be measured by GNP alone, many people have looked for a better, more comprehensive socio-economic measure. The human development index is a contribution to this search.

What does the HDI include?

The HDI is a composite of three basic components of human development: longevity, knowledge and standard of living. Longevity is measured by life expectancy. Knowledge is measured by a combination of adult literacy (two-thirds weight) and means years of schooling (one-third weight). Standard of living is measured by purchasing power, based on real GDP per capita adjusted for the local cost of living (purchasing power parity, or PPP).

Why only three components?

The ideal would be to reflect all aspect of human experience. The lack of data imposes some limits on this, and more indicators could perhaps be added as the information becomes available. But more indicators would not necessarily be better. Some might overlap with existing indicators: infant mortality, for example, is already reflected in life expectancy. And adding more variables could confuse the picture and detract from the main trends.

How to combine indicators measured in different units?

The measuring rod for GNP is money. The breakthrough for the HDI, however, was to find a common measuring rod for the socioeconomic distance travelled. The HDI sets a minimum and a maximum for each dimension and then shows where each country stands in relation to these scales – expressed as a value between 0 and 1. So, since the minimum adult literacy rate is 0 per cent and the maximum is 100 per cent, the literacy component of knowledge for a country where the literacy rate if 75 per cent would be 0.75. Similarly, the minimum for life expectancy is 25 years and the maximum 85 years, so the longevity component for a country where life expectancy is 55 years would be 0.5. For income the minimum is $200 (PPP) and the maximum is $40,000 (PPP). The scores for the three dimensions are then averaged in an overall index.

Is it not misleading to talk of a single HDI for a country with great inequality?

National averages can conceal much. The best solution would be to create separate HDIs for the most significant groups: by gender, for example, or by income group, geographical region, race or ethnic group. Separate HDIs would reveal a more detailed profile of human deprivation in each country, and disaggregated HDIs are already being attempted for countries with sufficient data.

How can the HDI be used?

The HDI offers an alternative to GNP for measuring the relative socio-economic progress of nations. It enables people and their governments to evaluate progress over time and to determine priorities for policy intervention. It also permits instructive comparisons of the experiences in different countries.

Source: UNDP, 1994

Table 2 HDI ranking for selected industrial and developing countries, 1997

	HDI value	HDI rank	Real GDP per capita (PPS$) rank minus HDI rank *
High human development			
Canada	0.932	1	12
Norway	0.927	2	5
United States	0.927	3	0
Japan	0.924	4	5
Belgium	0.923	5	6
Sweden	0.923	6	18
Australia	0.922	7	15
Netherlands	0.921	8	9
Iceland	0.919	9	3
United Kingdom	0.918	10	9
Singapore	0.888	22	−18
Hong King, China	0.880	24	−16
Korea, Rep. of	0.852	30	3
Kuwait	0.833	35	−30
United Arab Emirates	0.812	43	−18
Medium human development			
Mexico	0.786	50	−3
Malaysia	0.768	56	−7
Cuba	0.765	58	47
Thailand	0.753	67	−7
Saudi Arabia	0.740	78	−37
Jamaica	0.734	82	15
Turkey	0.728	86	−22
Sri Lanka	0.721	90	22
China	0.701	98	6
South Africa	0.695	101	−47
Vietnam	0.664	110	23
Egypt	0.616	120	−14
Botswana	0.609	122	−70
Zimbabwe	0.560	130	−16
India	0.545	132	− 1
Low human development			
Nepal	0.463	144	11
Nigeria	0.456	146	15
Bangladesh	0.440	150	6
Tanzania	0.421	156	16
Malawi	0.399	159	10
Mozambique	0.341	169	−2
Ethiopia	0.298	172	1
Sierra Leone	0.254	174	0

*A positive figure indicates that the HDI rank is better than the real GDP (PPP$) rank, a negative the opposite. The treatment of income was changed in the 1999 report, so HDIs for 1997 are not strictly comparable with previous years.

Source: UNDP, *Human Development Report 1999*

But not all poor countries have low HDIs. For many countries – Cuba, Vietnam, Sri Lanka and Tanzania, for example – HDI rankings are significantly above GDP rankings, indicating the priority that these countries attach to health and education, especially the education of women.

In other cases, the discrepancy between HDI and GDP rankings indicates that many countries with relatively high GDP *per capita* – Saudi Arabia, Kuwait, the United Arab Emirates, South Africa, Botswana and Singapore – have lower HDI rankings. These discrepancies are explained by various factors – income inequalities (as they affect access to healthcare and education in the case of South Africa, for example) and the position of women (Saudi Arabia). It is perhaps surprising to see that Singapore and Hong Kong, China, have HDI rankings significantly below their GDP *per capita* rankings (note female illiteracy in these two economies – Table 4).

A comparison of HDIs over time reveals some interesting trends and re-emphasizes the point made above that care needs to be exercised when making statements about the development process and experience. As Table 3 shows, all countries made substantial progress in human development over the period 1960–92. The overall HDI for

Table 3 HDI Values by region, 1960–92

	1960	1992	Absolute increase in HDI value 1960–92
All developing countries	0.260	0.541	0.281
Least developed countries	0.165	0.307	0.142
Industrial*	0.799	0.918	0.119
World	0.392	0.605	0.213
Sub-Saharan Africa	0.200	0.357	0.156
Middle East and North Africa	0.277	0.631	0.354
South Asia	0.202	0.376	0.174
East Asia	0.255	0.653	0.397
South-East Asia and Oceania	0.284	0.613	0.329
Latin America and the Caribbean	0.467	0.757	0.290
Excl. Mexico and Brazil	0.504	0.735	0.231

*Excluding Eastern Europe and the former Soviet Union

Source: UNDP, 1994

the least developed countries and those in sub-Saharan Africa increased by approximately 80 per cent, although they started from very low levels.

In East Asia, the HDI increased two and a half times over the same period, indicating that investment in human development is both a cause and consequence of rapid economic growth. It is interesting to compare trends in the HDI with *per capita* income. No country experienced a fall in its HDI over the period covered, and the UNDP concludes that *'Human capital, once it is built up, is more likely to be sustainable'*.

An index of human poverty

In 1997 the UNDP introduced the **Human Poverty Index** (HPI) in an attempt to bring together in a composite index the different dimensions of deprivation in human life. The *concept* of human poverty is greater than the *measure* – all its dimensions cannot be included in a single quantifiable composite indicator – but the HPI does draw attention to three essential elements already included in the HDI (longevity, knowledge and a decent standard of living).

Deprivation in longevity is represented by the percentage of people not expected to survive to age 40 years; deprivation of knowledge by the percentage of adults who are illiterate; and the deprivation in a decent standard of living is represented by a composite of the percentage of people without access to safe water, the percentage of people without access to health services, and the percentage of moderately and severely underweight children aged under 5 years.

The difference between the HDI and the HPI is that the former measures progress in a community or a country as a whole; the HPI measures the extent of deprivation, the proportion of people not benefiting from the development process. The UNDP has estimated the HPI for 77 developing countries. It ranges from 3 per cent in Trinidad to 62 per cent in Niger. It exceeds 50 per cent in Mali, Ethiopia, Sierra Leone, Burkino Faso and Niger.

A comparison of HDI and HPI values shows the extent to which the achievements of development are evenly distributed within a country. For example, China and Egypt have similar HDI values, but the HPI for China is only 17 per cent while the HPI for Egypt is 34 per cent. The fruits of human development are more equitably distributed in China than they are in Egypt. The HPI measure also shows that human poverty remains much higher than income poverty in many countries (for example, Egypt and Pakistan).

Table 4 Basic indicators

	Population (millions 1997)	GNP per capita $. 1997	GNP per capita Rank	GNP measured at PPP $. 1997	GNP measured at PPP Rank	Annual average growth GDP (%) 1980–90	Annual average growth GDP (%) 1990–97	Life expectancy at birth, 1996 Males	Life expectancy at birth, 1996 Females	Adult (aged 15 and above) Illiteracy rate, 1995 (%) Males	Adult (aged 15 and above) Illiteracy rate, 1995 (%) Females
Low-income economies											
Mozambique	19	90	133	520	121	1.7	6.9	44	46	42	77
Ethiopia	60	110	132	510	122	2.3	4.5	48	51	55	75
Tanzania	31	210	127	–	–	–	–	49	52	21	43
Malawi	10	220	124	700	118	2.3	3.6	43	43	28	58
Zimbabwe	11	750	85	2280	80	3.4	2.0	55	57	10	20
Sierra Leone	5	200	129	510	123	0.6	–3.3	35	38	55	82
Nigeria	118	260	119	880	114	1.6	2.7	51	55	33	53
Bangladesh	124	270	116	1050	106	4.3	4.5	57	59	51	74
Nepal	23	210	125	1090	103	4.6	5.0	57	57	59	86
India	961	390	102	1650	92	5.8	5.9	62	63	35	62
Pakistan	137	490	97	1590	94	6.3	4.4	62	65	50	76
Middle-income economies											
Lower-middle income											
China	1227	860	81	3570	65	10.2	11.9	68	71	10	27
Indonesia	200	1110	75	3450	67	6.1	7.5	63	67	10	22
Thailand	61	2800	50	6590	41	7.6	7.5	67	72	4	8
Bolivia	8	950	79	–	–	–2.0	3.8	59	63	10	24
Jamaica	3	1560	65	3470	66	2.0	0.8	72	77	19	11

	Population ($ millions 1997)	GNP per capita $ .1997	GNP per capita Rank	GNP measured at PPP $ .1997	GNP measured at PPP Rank	Annual average growth GDP (%) 1980–90	Annual average growth GDP (%) 1990–97	Life expectancy at birth, 1996 Males	Life expectancy at birth, 1996 Females	Adult (aged 15 and above) illiteracy rate, 1995 (%) Males	Adult (aged 15 and above) illiteracy rate, 1995 (%) Females
Peru	25	2460	53	4390	57	-0.3	6.0	66	71	6	17
Egypt, Arab rep.	60	1180	72	2940	72	5.3	3.9	64	67	36	61
Russian Federation	147	2740	51	4190	59	2.8	-9.0	60	73	–	–
Upper-middle income											
Turkey	64	3130	48	6430	43	5.3	3.6	66	71	8	28
Brazil	164	4720	34	6240	47	2.8	3.1	63	71	17	17
South Africa	38	3400	45	7490	37	1.2	1.5	62	68	18	18
Hungary	10	4430	37	7000	39	1.6	-0.4	65	75	–	–
Poland	39	3590	43	6380	46	1.8	3.9	68	77	–	–
Malaysia	21	4680	35	10920	29	5.2	8.7	70	74	11	22
High-income											
Korea,. Rep. of	46	10550	25	13500	24	9.5	7.2	69	76	1	3
Hong Kong, China	7	25280	13	24540	4	6.9	5.3	76	81	4	12
Singapore	3	32940	4	29000	1	6.6	8.5	74	79	4	14
United Kingdom	59	20710	15	20520	14	3.2	1.9	74	80	*	*
United States	268	28740	6	27840	2	2.9	2.5	74	80	*	*
Switzerland	7	44320	1	26320	3	2.2	-0.1	75	82	*	*
Japan	126	37850	2	23400	6	4.0	1.4	77	83	*	*
Germany	82	28260	7	21300	13	2.2	–	73	80	*	*

*According to UNESCO, illiteracy is less than 5 per cent; data not given.
Source: World Bank, *World Development Report*, 1999

Basic indicators

Table 4 gives some basic indicators for a sample of countries. The World Bank classifies countries as follows:

- low-income: *per capita* GNP of $785 or less in 1997
- lower-middle-income: *per capita* GNP less than $3125
- upper-middle-income: *per capita* GNP less than $9655
- high-income: *per capita* GNP above $9656.

The population of the low-income countries totalled 2.04 billion in 1997, with a *per capita* income of $350. The lower-middle-income group accounted for 2.285 billion people at a *per capita* income of $1230; and the upper-middle-income group accounted for 571 million at a *per capita* income of $4520. Overall, therefore, approximately five billion people lived in low- and middle-income economies in 1997, in comparison with about 926 million living in the high-income economies (with GNP *per capita* of $25 700).

The data in Table 4 permit a number of interesting comparisons to be made:

- Compare GNP *per capita* converted into US dollars at existing exchange rates with GNP measured at PPP. Note how the rankings change using these two methods (Switzerland is replaced by Singapore as the country with the highest *per capita* income when measured at PPP).
- Compare growth rates over the period 1980–90 with those for 1990–97. Note the improvement in some countries – for example, Mozambique and Peru – with the collapse of the Russian Federation in the 1990s.
- Compare life expectancy at birth between different countries and differences between male and female life expectancies. Note the low male life expectancy in the Russian Federation.
- Compare rates of illiteracy between countries. Note that Egypt's profile is closer to the lower-income economies. Note also the differential between male and female illiteracy rates (only Jamaica has a male illiteracy rate higher than that for females).

Conclusions

The search for a composite indicator of development will continue, even though it is recognized that it is virtually impossible to give every aspect of social progress a money value. Most economists would accept that information on how much is produced (GNP or GDP) must be supplemented by information on what is produced, by what means, for whom and with what impact. What is required, therefore, are indicators of the composition and beneficiaries of GNP/GDP which will supplement, but not replace, GNP/GDP data.

However, not everyone would agree with the notion of development as modernization, and the debate over the meaning of development is likely to be long-running.

KEY WORDS

Value judgements	Gross domestic product
Economic development	*Per capita* income
Sustainable development	Purchasing power parity
Intergenerational welfare	Human Development Index
Gross national product	Human Poverty Index

Further reading

Anderton, A., Unit 100 in *Economics*, 3rd edn, Causeway Press, 2000.

Atkinson, B., Livesey, F., and Milward, R. (eds), Chapter 27 in *Applied Economics*, Macmillan, 1998.

Grant, S., Chapter 4 in *Economic Growth and Business Cycles*, Heinemann Educational, 1999.

United Nations Development Programme, *Human Development Report*, Oxford University Press, 1999.

Useful websites

The Guardian: www.newsunlimited.co.uk

United Nations Conference on Trade and Development: www. unctad.org

United Nations Development Programme: www.undp.org

Essay topics

1. (a) Explain the difference between economic development and economic growth.   [8 marks]
   (b) How do economists measure economic development? [4 marks]
   (c) Comment upon the difficulties involved in such measurement.
                                                          [8 marks]

   [UCLES, June 1997]
2. Assess the extent to which changes in a country's GDP is a reliable indicator of changes in the living standards of the country's citizens.
                                                          [20 marks]

Data response question

This task is based on a question set by Edexcel in 1999. Study the data in Table A and then, using your knowledge of economics, answer all the questions that follow.

Table A *Per capita* income and several indicators of human welfare for 15 countries in the 1990s

Nation	GNP per capita, 1997 ($)	Life expectancy of males at birth, 1996 (years)	Infant mortality rate per 1000, 1996	Access to healthcare, 1990–95 (% population)
Ethiopia	110	48	177	46
Malawi	220	43	217	35
Burkina Faso	240	45	158	90
Bangladesh	270	57	112	45
Haiti	330	54	130	60
Kenya	330	57	90	77
Ghana	370	57	110	60
India	90	62	85	85
Nicaragua	410	65	57	83
Lesotho	670	57	113	80
Ivory Coast	690	53	150	30
Sri Lanka	800	71	19	93
China	860	68	39	88
Ecuador	1590	67	40	88
Mexico	3680	69	36	93

Sources: World Bank *World Development Report 1998/99*, OUP; UNDP *Human Development Report 1998*, OUP

1. (a) What do you understand by 'GNP *per capita*'? [2 marks]
   (b) Examine the difficulties of comparing standards of living in different countries using GNP *per capita* data. [6 marks]
2. Graph the data of *per capita* income and of life expectancy. Explain why a relationship between these two variables might be expected. [5 marks]
3. With reference to the data, examine the factors which might explain the difference in life expectancy and infant mortality rates. [6 marks]
4. Explain why expenditure on healthcare in developing countries might be regarded as one form of investment spending. [6 marks]

Chapter Three

Development theory

'If development economics is to have credibility, there must be a commonality among the countries it studies, a unity in diversity.'
Barbara Ingham, University of Salford

Characteristics of less-developed countries

As we have seen, the notion of a 'Third World' is based on the presumption that poor, less-developed countries (LDCs) share a set of common economic, social, political and institutional characteristics. By 'adding-up' such characteristics, some economists have attempted to explain the origins of poverty and its persistence over time.

In one of the most widely used textbooks (Michael Todaro, *Economic Development*, 5th edn, Longman, 1994) the common characteristics of LDCs are listed thus:

- low levels of living, comprising low incomes, high inequality, poor health and inadequate education;
- low levels of productivity;
- high rates of population growth and dependency burdens;
- significant dependence on agricultural production and primary-product exports;
- dominance, dependence and vulnerability in international relations.

At the same time, there is great diversity both within and between LDCs, with respect to their historical experiences and their contemporary economic performance. For example, while it is true that the great majority of poor countries were at one time colonies of the metropolitan powers (Spain, Portugal, Netherlands, France, Belgium, the UK and, at a later stage, Japan), the impact and consequences of colonial rule varied widely between countries and over time.

More recently, most poor countries have attempted to industrialize. Some have achieved great success in the endeavour (the economies of East and South East Asia), while others (the majority of the economies of sub-Saharan Africa) have not yet succeeded. There are huge differences in population size, and increasingly – given the differences in rates of economic growth between countries – in *per capita* incomes.

Differences in resource endowments also exist, with some of the poorest countries (the Democratic Republic of Congo and Angola, for example) having great natural resource endowments.

Given the diversity of experience, endowment and performance, we must be careful not to oversimplify theories and explanations of underdevelopment and development. Of necessity, economists have to simplify and generalize in order to construct theories which give them testable hypotheses. But we must not lose sight of the historical and global dimensions of development, and the need for new – and perhaps unorthodox – explanations for the persistence of poverty and inequality.

Introduction to the theory

The theoretical origins of development economics as a sub-discipline are remarkably diverse. They were:

- the 'Keynesian revolution', with its justification of government intervention in order to achieve macroeconomic targets;
- early growth theory, especially the Harrod–Domar model (see below);
- the experience of wartime planning and intervention in the economy in the UK and the USA;
- the example of the Soviet Union's rapid industrialization in the 1930s;
- decolonization – the concern with economic development of political parties campaigning for independence in the colonies and planning by governments in newly independent states (e.g. India).

This diversity of theoretical inputs, historical experience and political expediency has meant that development economists, while using the tools of orthodox economic analysis, have nevertheless often been highly unorthodox in their approach to development problems. Nevertheless, most have shared a number of common concerns.

- Attention has been focused on the long run, with economic growth usually taking priority over considerations of static allocative efficiency.
- Economic growth and changes in the structure of output, employment and consumption, and patterns of trade, have been closely linked to one another.
- The focus has been on savings and investment (accumulation) and the policies and institutions required to encourage and sustain the accumulation process.
- The development of human resources, through expenditure on health and education, has always been seen as an important aspect of the development process (human capital formation).

- Alternative development strategies – some highly unorthodox – have been given serious consideration and have often influenced the policymaking process.

Alternative theoretical perspectives on development

Development economists have perhaps been more prepared than others to recognize the need for, and the existence of, a variety of theoretical approaches to the study of economic development. Economists discussing development therefore consider differing questions, and as a result come up with differing answers and – most importantly – differing policy recommendations. For the sake of simplicity, we can identify three schools of thought: orthodox, structuralist and radical.

The orthodox school

The **orthodox** (sometimes referred to as **neoclassical**) school focuses attention on the *efficiency* with which resources are allocated. Unnecessary government intervention in product and factor markets gives rise to 'distorted' relative prices, because (i) limits on interest rates make capital too 'cheap', (ii) minimum-wage legislation raises wages above their market clearing level, and (iii) tariffs imposed on imported commodities raise domestic prices above international prices. This in turn gives rise to a misallocation of resources because industry is overprotected, relative to agriculture for example.

The World Bank's recommendation that countries should 'get prices right' illustrates the view that markets lead to the most efficient resource allocation, and that government intervention should be confined to the provision of macroeconomic stability, security to the owners of property, and any action necessary to overcome market failures. World Bank policies in the 1980s illustrate the application of orthodox macro- and microeconomic policies.

The structuralist school

The **structuralist** school of thought emerged largely in Latin America after World War II, principally as a reaction to what were seen as irrelevant orthodox theories.

Structuralists argued that LDCs were characterized by a variety of constraints, which meant that either markets did not exist or that markets operated imperfectly – with outcomes that were considered undesirable.

For example, it was argued that the growth of incomes and

urbanization would lead to an increase in demand for foodstuffs. This increase in demand, however, would not stimulate an increase in supply because of the structure of land ownership in the agricultural sector. The large estates (the *latifundia*) would not respond to higher prices because they were not profit-maximizers – land was held for social and political reasons as well as for economic ones. On the other hand the small landowners – the *minifundia* – were at the margins of subsistence and would not be able to take the risk of supplying the market for fear of jeopardizing their own survival. Land ownership was thus a **structural bottleneck**.

Other structuralist theories include the secular deterioration in the terms of trade of primary-product exporters (see Chapter 8), and the theory of import-substituting industrialization (see Chapter 7).

The radical school

The **radical** school of thought is less easy to characterize. Some economists have argued that poor countries will never develop as long as they remain a part of the global capitalist economy ('the development of underdevelopment', a slogan associated with the American economist Andre Gunder Frank).

Others – for example Fernando Henrique Cardoso, a leading Brazilian sociologist, now President of Brazil – have argued that only '**dependent development**' is possible, because of the subordinate position of poor countries in the global economy and the absence of key sectors in those economies (especially the low level of development of the machine-making sector – capital goods).

Yet others take the famous Marxist dictum: '*The country that is more developed industrially only shows to the less developed the image of its own future.*' They argue that capitalist development is occurring on a large scale in many areas of the Third World – as in East and South East Asia, and in parts of Latin America – and that what is needed is a strong government that is able to intervene on a selective basis in the economy in order to promote capital accumulation, both physical and human, and industrialization.

Balanced versus unbalanced growth

The theory of **balanced growth** was the outcome of the work of a number of different economists, and had its origins in the poorer peripheral economies of Eastern and South Eastern Europe in 1943.

Industrialization in that region was constrained by the small size of the domestic market, by the inability of firms to internalize the value of *external economies* that they generated – for example, the training of labour which might then leave to work for other firms – and by the inability of firms to anticipate the external economies generated by the investment of other firms.

If a number of consumer goods industries were established simultaneously, the workers in one factory would provide the market for the output of other factories. This was the idea behind the 'Big Push' theory of industrialization. It highlighted the need for state intervention – to invest in training the labour force, to plan and organize the large-scale investment programme, and to help mobilize the necessary finance. Balanced growth thus became associated with 'planning' and industrialization.

It quickly became apparent that a strategy of balanced growth was beyond the resources of most poor countries. First, both governments and domestic entrepreneurs would have to provide the impetus to growth. Secondly, the scale of the resource mobilization effort would have to be huge. Thirdly, the investment programme itself would have to be sufficiently large to overcome the diseconomies of small scale, to reduce the risks of market failure and to exploit external economies fully.

Critics of balanced growth thus argued that LDCs had neither the organizational nor the managerial skills to implement such a strategy and that **unbalanced growth** was more practicable.

Planners and policymakers would no longer attempt to anticipate supply and demand imbalances but would allow the market to reveal bottlenecks. The latter would then *induce* investment, from both the public and private sectors, to overcome them. The American economist Albert Hirschman, in particular, argued that governments should encourage investment in branches of production with significant **inter-industry linkages** – *backward* linkages to raw materials and input supplies, and *forward* linkages with users of the industry's output.

Rostow's stages of economic growth

In 1960, the American economist W. W. Rostow published a book entitled *The Stages of Growth: A Non-Communist Manifesto*. In it he argued that all countries experienced a similar sequence of development, and that countries differed with respect to the stage they were at at any point in time. The five stages he suggested were:

1. the traditional society
2. the transitional stage (the preconditions for take-off)
3. the take-off
4. the drive to maturity
5. the stage of high mass consumption

The rich industrialized market economies were in stages 4 and 5 while the poor countries were seen as being in stages 1 and 2. The latter, transitional stage, was a crucial one, during which there would occur changes in agriculture, transport and international trade, and entrepreneurs would emerge. This stage would be followed by the **take-off period**, of perhaps 10 to 20 years, during which rates of investment would double, leading economic sectors emerge and self-sustaining growth provide for the transition to stages 4 and 5.

The notion of a 'take-off period' was influential, but the stages theory has been subject to a number of criticisms:

- It is difficult to distinguish between the end of one stage and the beginning of the next.
- The stage of high mass consumption is not the 'end' of development – rich countries undergo structural change (deindustrialization), booms and slumps, and they differ among themselves (compare the UK and Japan).
- The notion of a traditional society, unchanging and common to all poor countries, is not valid.
- The condition of today's poor countries is different from that of the now-rich countries when they were at comparable levels of GNP *per capita*.

Logically, no country can replicate the development experience of another country, as the development of one country changes the economic environment within which other countries develop.

The Harrod–Domar model

Neither of the authors credited with the development of this model were concerned with developing countries, but it has been widely used by economic planners in the Third World.

Once a planner has a rough idea as to how many units of capital are required to produce one unit of output (the *incremental capital output ratio, k*), and the *savings ratio* is known, then the rate of growth of income can be calculated. Alternatively, if a target rate of growth (g) is set, then the required savings ratio (s) can be estimated for any given k (see the boxed item on page 33).

If it is assumed that *employment* growth is related in some predictable way to *output* growth, this model also gives employment predictions or indicates the rates of growth that must be attained in order to reach employment targets.

However, a number of criticisms can be made of the model:

- Is it the level of savings that restricts investment, or is it the lack of profitable investment opportunities that restricts savings?
- The original model assumes a **closed economy,** but once foreign trade is introduced the major constraint on economic growth might well be the availability of foreign exchange rather than domestic savings.

THE HARROD-DOMAR MODEL

Saving (S) is some proportion (s) of national income (Y) such that

$$S = sY \quad \text{(equation 1)}.$$

Investment (I) is defined as the change (delta) in the capital stock (K), represented as delta K, such that

$$I = \Delta K \quad \text{(equation 2)}.$$

The capital stock (K) bears a fixed relationship to national income or output (Y) as expressed by the capital–output ratio (k), such that

$$\frac{K}{Y} = k$$

or

$$\frac{\Delta K}{\Delta Y} = k \quad \text{(equation 3)}.$$

In equilibrium, savings equals investment:

$$S = I.$$

Therefore $sY = k\Delta Y$ from equations (1), (2) and (3), and $s/k = \Delta Y/Y = g$, where g is the growth of national income.
An example: If s = 12 per cent and k = 3, then g = 4 per cent.

The accompanying production possibility curve summarizes the importance of capital growth. I is the change in the capital stock, K. The national income, Y, increases if consumption, C, is reduced, in the short run, from C_a to C_b, to release saving, S, and resources for additional I, from I_a to I_b.

In the long run, the increase in the economy's capacity shifts the production possibility frontier outwards to the pecked line which can then allow both higher C and higher I.

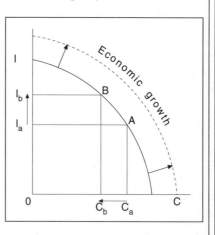

- Is the capital–output ratio fixed? Neoclassical economists would argue that capital and labour will be substituted for one another depending on their relative prices, hence influencing k.
- k will vary between different sectors of the economy (it may be lower in agriculture, for example, than in industry) and thus growth will in part be determined by the distribution of investment between sectors.

The vicious circle of poverty

The idea of a **vicious circle** of poverty is closely associated with the work of Ragnar Nurkse who published his influential book *Problems of Capital Formation in Underdeveloped Countries* in 1953.

Nurkse argued that a vicious circle was a 'circular constellation of forces tending to act and react upon one another in such a way as to keep a poor country in a state of poverty'. The most widely quoted example of a vicious circle is with respect to capital accumulation. The low level of real income in 'underdeveloped areas' resulted in a limited capacity to save and was itself a reflection of low productivity. Low productivity in turn was the result of the lack of capital which was the result of the limited capacity to save. The circle was thus complete (see Figure 2).

On the demand side, the inducement to invest may be low because of the limited size of the market, itself the result of low real income resulting from low productivity. Productivity is low because of the limited use of capital in production which in turn may be at least partly caused by the low inducement to invest (see Figure 3).

The notion of a vicious circle is intuitively appealing, but it is in fact static and goes against the evidence of history. Low-income economies have broken out or escaped from their vicious circles of poverty (for example, Singapore and the Republic of Korea) and savings may well be determined by the distribution of income (as in the **Lewis model** –

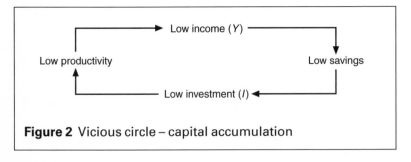

Figure 2 Vicious circle – capital accumulation

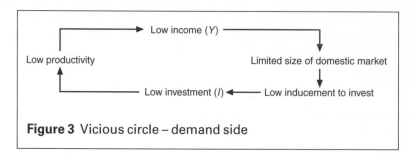

Figure 3 Vicious circle – demand side

see below) rather than its level. The possibilities for trade overcome the limitations of the domestic market (see Chapter 8), and direct foreign investment (Chapter 9) and international aid (Chapter 10) may well provide the financial and other inputs required to kick-start and sustain the process of growth and development.

The Lewis model

The Lewis model, published in *The Manchester School* in 1954 ('Economic development with unlimited supplies of labour') has probably been the most influential model in development economics. Drawing on the historical experience of western industrialized economies, and on the ideas of the classical economists (for example, not all factors are scarce – labour is in unlimited supply), Sir Arthur Lewis derived a very general picture of the development process.

The model describes the transfer of surplus labour from a low-productivity non-capitalist subsistence sector (usually taken to mean agriculture) to a high-productivity capitalist sector (usually taken to mean the industrial sector).

At an early stage of development in many countries, Lewis argued, there is surplus labour in the subsistence economy, so that the supply of labour to the capitalist sector will exceed demand at a constant wage rate. The wage rate in the capitalist sector is equal to average product in the subsistence sector, plus perhaps an extra 30 per cent to induce labour transfer and to compensate for higher capitalist sector living costs.

Figure 4 illustrates the basic Lewis model. As economic growth proceeds (indicated by the movement of the MP of labour schedule from N_1D_1 to N_2D_2 and so on) the re-investment of profits will lead to the growth of the capitalist sector both in absolute and relative terms (that is, the capitalist sector will grow relatively faster than the subsistence sector). Because of the constant wage, the share of profits in

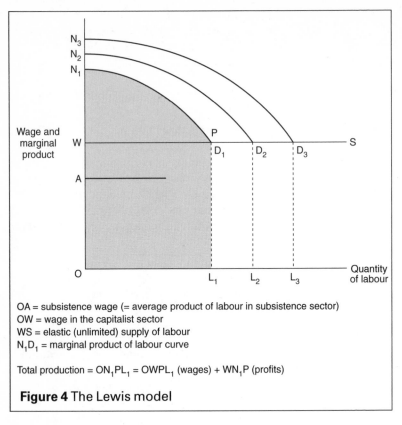

OA = subsistence wage (= average product of labour in subsistence sector)
OW = wage in the capitalist sector
WS = elastic (unlimited) supply of labour
N_1D_1 = marginal product of labour curve

Total production = ON_1PL_1 = $OWPL_1$ (wages) + WN_1P (profits)

Figure 4 The Lewis model

national income is likely to rise; and given that a higher proportion of profit income is saved and invested than is the case with other incomes, the savings ratio and capital accumulation will rise, on which economic development depends.

Many have taken this to mean that income distribution must inevitably worsen as development proceeds. But a rising share of profits in national income could be offset by a fall in the share of rents. What is important is the savings behaviour of the recipients of increasing income – the capitalists (or the state if productive assets are publicly owned) are assumed to save whilst landowners are assumed to consume.

Once surplus labour is exhausted and wages rise, this first 'classical phase' of the development process comes to an end. With the supply of labour inelastic we enter a neoclassical world where all factors are scarce.

The Lewis model has generated much debate and criticism. But its supporters argue that it was mainly intended to shed light on historical change and that it remains an illuminating framework within which to discuss the process of economic development.

Planning and markets
Over the past two decades, ideas on economic policies for development have changed dramatically.

- First, the results of attempts at economic planning have in general been disappointing. The collapse of the previously planned economies of eastern and central Europe and the former Soviet Union has further discredited the notion that resources can be allocated more efficiently by the state than by markets.
- Public sectors have been overexpanded. In many countries this has led to the creation of overstaffed, inefficient, loss-making enterprises.
- Governments have allowed public spending to exceed revenue, leading to excessive borrowing, increases in money supply and aggravation of inflationary pressures.

The 1980s saw a change in emphasis in development policy, with the following coming to the top of the agenda:

- **liberalization**, especially of trade;
- **structural adjustment**;
- **privatization**.

A more limited role for government was envisaged focusing on:

- proper macroeconomic management of the economy;
- the creation of an efficient regulatory and promotional framework;
- investment in education and health (human capital) and infrastructure (physical capital);
- protection of poor and vulnerable members of society.

Conclusions
Most development economists would now accept that governments must try to create a 'market friendly' environment in order to encourage economic development. The recognition that poor countries share common characteristics and face similar problems gives a 'unity in diversity' to the study of development problems. This should not, however, obscure their diversity and the need to design policies that reflect the often unique characteristics of individual countries.

> ## KEY WORDS
>
> | | |
> |---|---|
> | Keynesian revolution | Balanced growth |
> | Harrod–Domar model | Unbalanced growth |
> | Allocative efficiency | Inter-industry linkages |
> | Accumulation | Take-off period |
> | Human capital formation | Closed economy |
> | Orthodox/neoclassical | Vicious circle |
> | Structuralist | Lewis model |
> | Structural bottleneck | Liberalization |
> | Radical | Structural adjustment |
> | Dependent development | Privatization |

Further reading
Anderton, A., Unit 102 in *Economics*, 3rd edn, Causeway Press, 2000.

Cook, M., and Healey, N., Chapter 2 in *Supply Side Economics*, 4th edn, Heinemann Educational, 2000.

Grant, S., Chapter 3 in *Economic Growth and Business Cycles*, Heinemann Educational, 1999.

Todaro, M., Chapters 1–3 in *Economic Development*, 5th edn, Longman, 1994.

Useful websites
The Economist: www.economist.com

World Bank Statistics: www.worldbank.org/data

Essay topics
1. (a) Describe the Harrod–Domar model of growth. [6 marks]
   (b) With the use of economic theory, discuss the policies a government might introduce to promote economic development.
   [14 marks]
   [UCLES, June 1998]
2. (a) Describe the characteristics of developing countries. [10 marks]
   (b) Discuss how relevant Rostow's stages of growth are to the decisions of economic policymakers in developing countries.
   [10 marks]

Data response question
This task is based on a question set by OCR in 2000. The World Bank, as part of its policy to promote development, encourages economic

reform. This often involves the move from an economy controlled by the government to one where competitive markets operate.

The two diagrams on page 40 are adapted from a World Bank publication. Figure A shows the position before reform and Figure B that after changes have been made. The labels at the bottom of each describe the state of each sector. In both diagrams the relationships between different sectors are shown by the direction and size of the arrows. Study the diagrams and then answer the questions.

1. If an economy undergoes the process of reform shown in Figures A and B, identify:
   (a) the type of organization which will disappear from the economy;
   [1 mark]
   (b) the additional source of revenue for the government.   [1 mark]
2. Use Figures A and B to describe how the roles of the government and of the private sector will change after implementation of the reforms favoured by the World Bank.   [4 marks]
3. (a) What do the reforms imply for savings and consumption?
   [2 marks]
   (b) Explain briefly why economists believe that the savings ratio is important in economic development.   [3 marks]
4. Explain *one* economic change which would help to create the attractive business environment identified in Figure B.
5. Discuss the extent to which it is appropriate for developing economies to adopt the market-based economic systems of the developed countries.   [6 marks]

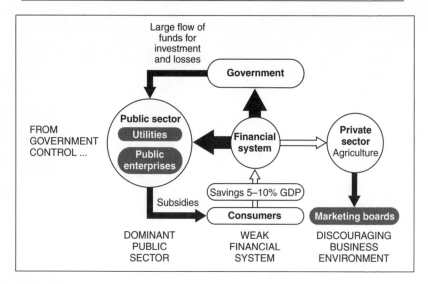

Figure A

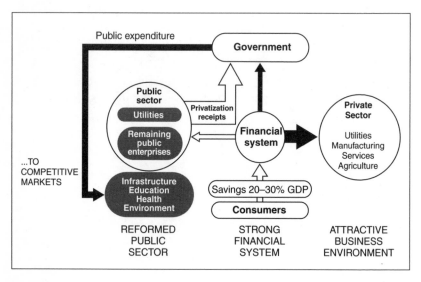

Figure B

Chapter Four

The global economy and the Third World

'... *the actual extent of global shifts in economic activity is extremely uneven. Only a small number of developing countries have experienced substantial economic growth; a good many are in deep financial difficulty whilst others are at, or even beyond, the margins of survival ... although we can indeed think in terms of a new international division of labour, its extent is far more limited than is sometimes claimed.*' Peter Dicken, *Global Shift: Transforming the World Economy*, 1998

There are huge inequalities in the global distribution of income, manufacturing production and international trade:

- Four-fifths of world manufacturing production is located in North America, western Europe and Japan.
- Three countries alone – the USA, Japan and Germany – account for 60 per cent of global manufacturing production.
- Three-quarters of all world merchandise exports originate in the developed market economies, and approximately 60 per cent of this trade is between the developed market economies.
- Over 65 per cent of all exports of services originate in the developed market economies.
- The developed market economies are the dominant source of transnational investment (92 per cent of the total) and also the dominant destination (see Chapter 9). (All data have been taken from Dicken, 1998.)

This concentration of economic activity in the 'core' developed market economies has been described as the 'Triad'. If we include Mexico with North America (the North American Free Trade Area – NAFTA) and the rapidly growing economies of East and South East Asia with Japan, we have the situation in which more and more of global productive activity, trade and direct investment is being 'sucked in' to the Triad. This is illustrated in Figure 5.

Globalization may thus essentially consist of greater economic interdependence between the three pillars of the Triad, accelerated by

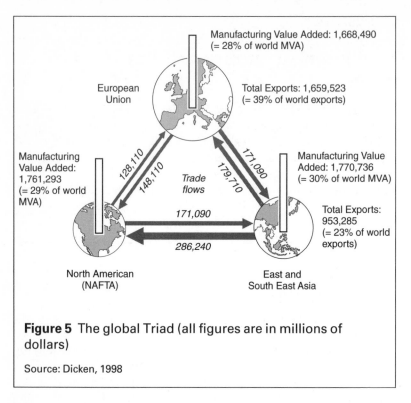

Figure 5 The global Triad (all figures are in millions of dollars)

Source: Dicken, 1998

liberalization, deregulation and the privatization of economic activities but largely excluding the rest of the world.

Inequalities in the global distribution of income appear to be increasing over time. UNDP (1999) notes that world inequalities have been rising for nearly two centuries. The distance between the richest and poorest countries was about 3 to 1 in 1973 and 72 to 1 in 1992. Obviously some countries have 'caught up' over this period – Japan, the countries of southern Europe, some Arab states, Singapore, Hong Kong, Republic of Korea and a number of other East and South East Asian economies – but, in general, divergence of *per capita* incomes, rather than convergence, appears to be the norm.

What is globalization?
Globalization is a multi-dimensional process of transformation which has many different meanings and interpretations. It generally refers both to the increasing flow of goods and resources across national boundaries and to the emergence of a complementary set of

organizational structures to manage the expanding network of international economic activity and transactions. *A stricter definition of globalization would be the emergence of a global economy where firms and financial institutions operate transnationally – that is, beyond the confines of national boundaries.* Differing interpretations of globalization carry varying emphasis.

- In one interpretation there is the development of global capital markets and large and volatile movements of short-term capital, the result of the liberalization of balance-of-payments capital account transactions (as in the build-up to the Asian financial crisis).
- In another interpretation there is the domination of the global economy by huge **transnational corporations** (TNCs) in key economic sectors – automobiles, media, entertainment and leisure, pharmaceuticals, financial services, telecommunications and information technology (IT).
- Others emphasize the increased interdependence between economies through international trade and direct foreign investment (DFI) (so-called 'shallow integration').
- Then there is the globalization of consumption through the development of global brands and trademarks – soft drinks, cigarettes, clothing and footwear, music, etc.
- Others stress the emergence of cross-border value-adding activities within TNCs and within networks established by TNCs which reinforce linkages between national economies (see Figure 6). This is so-called 'deep integration' in which technological change in general, and the development of IT in particular, play key roles. Note that this interpretation of globalization sees it as a *microeconomic* phenomenon, rather than as macroeconomic change.
- Broader conceptualizations of globalization would encompass issues relating to the environment (global warming), security and the spread of liberal democracy.

Many writers are critical of the more extreme versions of globalization, such as those predicting the end of the nation state. They argue that (i) a highly internationalized economy is not unprecedented, because the late nineteenth and early twentieth centuries were also a period of rapid global change; (ii) genuinely transnational corporations with no national base are rare; and (iii) there has been no massive shift of investment and employment to the Third World (that is, there is no 'new' international division of labour).

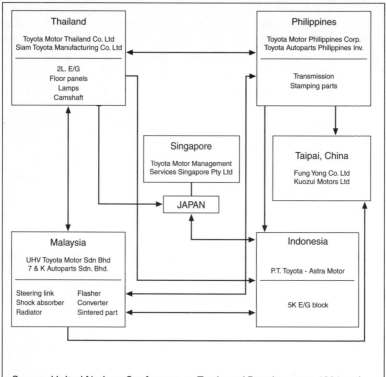

Source: United Nations Conference on Trade and Development, 1994 and 1996.

Figure 6 Toyota's network for auto parts in South East Asia

It is also necessary to point to the fact that, on any definition, the process of globalization is incomplete. There is no global labour market, except perhaps in certain occupations or activities – medicine, software engineering and football, for example; there is as yet no global taxation system aimed at improving the efficiency and fairness with which global resources are allocated; and there is no global system of regulation with respect to market structures and the behaviour (conduct) of global enterprises. The Geneva-based United Nations Conference on Trade and Development (UNCTAD) in 1997 argued for the use of the term 'global economic interdependence' rather than globalization, to indicate that the latter is not complete and that nation-states remain distinct economic identities with decision-making powers. UNCTAD argues that global economic forces can clearly bring potential benefits to low-income economies. The main issue is how to manage the interaction of domestic and international economic forces so that global economic interdependence leads to faster economic growth and rising living standards in those countries.

The **International Monetary Fund** (IMF) (1997) argues that countries that align themselves with the forces of globalization and implement the necessary economic reforms are likely to converge with the advanced economies (Republic of Korea, Singapore, Taiwan and Israel are quoted as examples of such countries). Countries which do not adopt such policies are likely to face declining shares of world trade and private capital/flows and will fall behind, in relative terms, the advanced countries. What the IMF in effect is saying is that if countries do not benefit from globalization, it is their own fault.

UNDP (1999, pp. 43–4) argues:

> '*Globalization expands the opportunities for unprecedented human advance for some but shrinks those opportunities for others and erodes human security. It is integrating economy, culture and governance but fragmenting societies. Driven by commercial market forces, globalization in this era seeks to promote economic efficiency, generate growth and yield profits. But it misses out on the goals of equity, poverty eradication and enhanced human security.*'

There is little evidence as yet that globalization is leading to convergence (that is, reductions in levels of *per capita* income or productivity) between rich and poor countries. Divergence – that is, increasing inequalities between rich and poor countries – appears to be the norm and it remains an open question as to whether this is in effect inherent in the globalization process itself (that is, it excludes poor countries as UNCTAD and UNDP seem to imply) or that it is poor policy in those countries that is to blame (the IMF's position).

The institutions of globalization

The major institutions of the globalized or increasingly economically interdependent global economy are the IMF, the **World Bank** (WB) and the World Trade Organization (WTO – discussed in Chapter 8). An attempt was made to establish a Multilateral Agreement of Investment (MAI) under the auspices of the Organization for Economic Co-operation and Development (OECD) in Paris in 1998. That attempt failed, and responsibility for future efforts at creating a new MAI has been transferred to the WTO in Geneva.

Both the IMF and the WB were established at the International Monetary and Financial Conference of the United and Associated nations at Bretton Woods (USA) in 1944. The IMF was to be mainly concerned with the provision of an adequate supply of international liquidity so that countries experiencing short-term balance of payments disequilibria would not have to resort to protectionist measures, thus maintaining an effective mechanism for international adjustment and stability. Since the early 1980s, the IMF has devoted most of its attention and resources to low-income economies with balance of payments problems through **stabilization programmes** negotiated with those countries. Special concessionary facilities were created for poor countries, renamed the Poverty Reduction and Growth Facility (PRGF) in 1999.

The World Bank (properly two legally and financially distinct entities – the International Bank for Reconstruction and Development and the International Development Association) was concerned initially with reconstruction of the war-torn economies of Europe, but from 1949 onwards its priorities shifted towards the promotion of economic development in what became the Third World. The IDA was established in 1960 as the soft-loan arm of the IBRD. Since the 1980s, the WB has increasingly been concerned with programme loans to poor countries (previously its activities had largely been based on projects) under the general headings of **structural adjustment**, or **sectoral adjustment, programmes**.

In reality the two sets of programmes appear to be similar. Both the IMF and the WB attach conditions to their loans to ensure that recipients meet certain agreed targets, pursue specified policies or implement agreed institutional changes. There is often 'cross-conditionality' between the two institutions (that is, the WB will not agree to a loan unless there is already an IMF stabilization programme in place).

A typical stabilization programme will consist of:

- monetary and fiscal contraction to reduce the public sector budget deficit in order to reduce aggregate demand (deflation);
- devaluation of the exchange rate;
- liberalization of the economy via the elimination of controls and regulations, privatization, trade liberalization (removal of quotas and rationalization and reduction of tariffs);
- wage restraint, removal of subsidies and reduction of transfer payments (but often accompanied by establishment of a 'social safety net').

A typical structural adjustment programme may well include all or some of the above measures, but will also include:

- measures to strengthen capacity to manage the public investment programme;
- revised agricultural pricing policies;
- revised industrial incentives;
- reform of the budget and tax system;
- improvement of export incentives.

The IMF and the WB come in for much criticism, not all of it justified. It is likely that we will see these institutions evolving and adapting over time to the changing global economy and the new problems those changes throw up.

Global instability

The small economic size and limited economic influence of most poor countries means that they are highly vulnerable to developments within the global economy which are beyond their control but which may have an adverse impact on their income, employment and prospects for economic growth.

The past three decades have been characterized by instability in the global economy.

- The early to mid 1970s witnessed the breakdown of the postwar system of fixed exchange rates (the Bretton Woods system), followed by two oil price shocks (1974/75 and 1979/80) and inflation and recession.
- The 1980s were characterized by slow economic growth, continued economic instability and growing disparities in economic performance between countries. The decade ended with the 'revolutions' in eastern and central Europe in 1989, and in 1990 there was the dissolution of the Council for Mutual Economic Assistance (the CMEA or COMECON) which was the 'common market' between the Soviet Union and its eastern and central European allies.
- The 1980s was a decade of crisis for the developing countries as a whole, and the period is often referred to as the 'lost decade'. It was subjected to a series of major **external shocks** (see the boxed item 'What are external shocks') in the early 1980s, and the continuation of adverse factors throughout the period made economic recovery difficult for many countries.

Excluding the transitional economies, however, there was an improvement in the growth performance of poor countries in the 1990s, largely the result of the rapid growth of the East Asia and Pacific group of countries. This region includes the original 'Gang of Four' –

WHAT ARE EXTERNAL SHOCKS?

The external shocks that most affected the developing countries were largely caused by the slowdown in global economic activity, especially in the early 1980s, which affected economic and industrial development through a number of channels:

- a reduction in demand for the developing countries' commodity and mineral exports;
- as a consequence, a fall in commodity prices and a reduction in the net barter terms of trade (see Chapter 7);
- a significant rise in global real interest rates, leading to an increase in the real burden of interest and debt repayments of poor debtor countries (see Chapter 10);
- a fall in the quantity of official development assistance (aid) and other capital flows to developing countries, resulting in negative net transfer of resources in 1984 and subsequent years for Latin America and Africa;
- increased vulnerability to rapid and significant changes in **short-term capital movements** in the late 1990s.

Singapore, Hong Kong, Taiwan and South Korea – as well as a number of other rapidly growing **newly industrializing economies,** or NIEs: Malaysia, Thailand, Indonesia and China.

The Asian financial crisis of 1997 and the subsequent crises in Russia in August 1998 and in Brazil (January 1999) introduced new elements of instability in the global economy, largely the result of many countries liberalizing their balance-of-payments capital accounts and thus becoming vulnerable to massive inflows and outflows of short-term capital (so-called 'hot money').

The Asian economies in general have recovered from the crisis, and the fear of contagion from the Russian and Brazilian crises appears in retrospect to have been exaggerated. But underlying problems persist. There remains potential instability inherent in the dependence of so many developing countries on volatile foreign capital inflows (UNCTAD, 1999).

The Asian financial crisis

The Asian financial crisis of 1997 was one of the most serious financial crises since the end of World War II. It was largely unexpected, hit a number of rapidly growing and highly successful economies, and promoted the largest financial bailout in history, stretching IMF resources to their limit.

The crisis began in Thailand in July 1997 with the devaluation of the Thai baht, following downwards pressure on the baht and the collapse of a number of key companies in the Thai financial sector. The contagion quickly spread to a number of other economies – the Philippines, Malaysia and Indonesia and finally the Republic of Korea – and exchange rates were floated and allowed to depreciate. (Note that other Asian economies – India, Pakistan, China and Taiwan – were either less or not affected by the crisis.) The IMF intervened early in the crisis and agreed rescue packages with Thailand, Indonesia and Korea. Malaysia did not agree to a programme with the IMF; and the Philippines, less affected than the other countries, was already in an IMF programme which was subsequently extended. Singapore and Hong Kong, China were hit by the crisis in 1998.

There are two basic interpretations of the causes of the crisis:

- The majority view (including that of the IMF) focused on structural problems and fundamental weaknesses in the Asian economies – large and persistent trade and current account deficits, loss of external competitiveness, excessive government intervention in these economies, 'crony capitalism', and problems of moral hazard (which arises when the incentives surrounding actions are distorted by the existence of explicit or implicit guarantees against loss).
- The second interpretation argues that although there were weaknesses and underlying problems in the Asian economies, they were essentially sound but *under-regulated*, especially with respect to their financial sectors, and that it was financial panic that was the basic element in the Asian crisis. Panic among the international investment community, policy mistakes at the onset of the crisis by Asian governments, and poorly designed international rescue programmes turned short-term capital inflows into a fully fledged financial panic and deepened the crisis.

The countries most affected by the crisis (Thailand, Malaysia, Indonesia and Korea) had liberalized capital account transactions and deregulated their financial sectors without putting in place the necessary framework of *prudential regulation*. Net private capital flows into the five most affected countries had risen from US$37.9 billion in 1994 to US$97.1 billion in 1996. These inflows suddenly reversed in the second half of 1997, turning to an outflow of US$11.9 billion, a turnaround of approximately US$109 billion (about 10 per cent of pre-crisis GDPs of these economies). Economies that had not practised **capital account liberalization** of transactions (China) or only partially liberalized them (Taiwan) were less affected by the crisis.

The consequences of the crisis included:

- a negative impact of the external trade of these economies (with knock-on effects for their major trading partners);
- falls in output, increases in bankruptcies and rises in unemployment;
- sharp rises in prices, especially those for basic necessities (foodstuffs and medicines);
- cuts in public expenditure as part of IMF stabilization programmes
- the erosion of the social fabric – political and social unrest in Indonesia, for example, increased poverty and inequality, with rises in crime.

The role of the IMF has come under increased scrutiny as a result of the crisis. Critics argue that it misinterpreted the causes of the crisis, insisted on a too-deflationary policy package to rescue the economies, and has in effect (some would say with the backing of the US Treasury) forced these countries, especially Korea, to deregulate and liberalize their economies, especially the financial sector, to encourage greater openness and foreign investment. The heavy indebtedness of the Korean chaebol has already led to significant sales of assets to foreign investors and massive restructuring. It is unlikely that the Korean state will be able or wish to play a significant developmental role in the future as it has in the past (see Chapter 7) and there has been a massive increase in inflows of direct foreign investment into Korea and Thailand in particular (as foreign companies buy up relatively cheap assets and/or invest in sectors of the economy from which they were previously restricted from entry).

The IMF has defended its role and has pointed to the stabilization of exchange rates and the rapidity of the recovery as evidence of success. It is also the case, of course, that we do not know what would have happened *if* there had been no IMF or IMF intervention. We have no *counterfactual* of what might have been.

Conclusions

The small *economic* size of the majority of poor countries makes them extremely vulnerable to adverse changes in global economic conditions. Some economies have been able to adjust to changed circumstances and have sustained long periods of rapid economic growth. Others have been unable to adjust and face economic stagnation and social and political crisis.

Economists disagree as to what factors determine a country's ability to adjust. Orthodox economists emphasize the importance of *free trade* and *the market* in reallocating resources and making an economy open to competitive pressures. Others point to the role of the '**developmental state**' in the East Asian context (see Chapter 7) and emphasize the importance of selective intervention by governments to ensure the achievement of development objectives.

Development economists quite properly continue to focus attention on issues of global poverty, inequality and instability. The western media often present an image of the Third World that reinforces popular notions of *famine and crisis*. There is, however, great diversity within the 'developing world' with respect to history, political evolution, institutions, and growth and development performance. It would be misleading to ignore the profound changes that are occurring in the global economy.

Nevertheless the forces of globalization and greater economic interdependence are creating both new opportunities and new problems for less-developed countries. New policies are needed to take advantage of those opportunities. New institutions are needed to attempt to deal with the fresh problems.

KEY WORDS

Globalization
Transnational corporations
International Monetary Fund
World Bank
Stabilization programme
Structural adjustment
   programmes

External shocks
Newly industrializing
   economies
Short-term capital movements
Capital account liberalization
Developmental state

Further reading

Atkinson, B., Livesey, F., and Milward, R. (eds), Chapter 28 in *Applied Economics*, Macmillan, 1998.

Bamford, C., and Grant, S., Chapter 8 in *The UK Economy in a Global Context*, Heinemann Educational, 2000.

Grant, S., Chapter 9 in *Economic Growth and Business Cycles*, Heinemann Educational, 1999.

Nixson, F., and Walters, B., 'The Asian crisis: causes and consequences', *Manchester School*, vol. 67, no. 5 (special issue).

Useful websites
International Monetary Fund: www.imf.org/
World Bank: www.worldbank.org/

Essay topics
1. (a) Explain the roles of the World Bank and IMF in economic development. [10 marks]
   (b) Discuss how the roles of the World Bank and IMF may change with globalization. [10 marks]
2. (a) Explain what is meant by external shocks. [6 marks]
   (b) Assess the impact an economic recession in the USA and EU would have on developing countries. [14 marks]

Data response question
This task is based on a question set by Edexcel in a specimen paper in 2000. Read the article, which is adapted from 'Africa: a flicker of light' published in *The Economist* on 5 March 1994. Then answer the questions.

The economics of sub-Saharan Africa

Africa has lurched backwards at a time when poor countries elsewhere have sprung ahead. Today the total wealth of Africa, with twice the population of the United States, is little more than that of Belgium. As recently as the mid-1980s, Africa's disastrous performance could be blamed chiefly on the folly of its leaders' economic policies. These policies involved extensive state intervention which had results which were the opposite of those intended. Policies included state marketing boards for agricultural products, over-valued exchange rates, import tariffs and quota controls, and state-run industrial enterprises. The many detailed forms of government intervention in the economy provided much scope for the corruption of civil servants.

In recent years, however, parts of Africa have been trying to introduce their most radical adjustments since independence. Some 30 African countries have abandoned their experiments with socialism – usually after pressure from foreign creditors – in favour of the free-market policies advocated by the World Bank and IMF. These policies have been very controversial. Britain's Oxfam, which has worked for decades in Africa, told the World Bank and IMF last September that structural adjustment 'can only be judged a complete failure.'

The World Bank is due to publish shortly its biggest study yet of adjustment in 29 sub-Saharan countries. It asks two main questions.

How much of what these countries promised did they actually do? And was the result a better economic performance in 1987–91 compared with 1981–86?

The news is not all bad. The Bank judges that six countries got the macroeconomic fundamentals right: Ghana, Tanzania, Gambia, Burkina Faso, Nigeria and Zimbabwe. On average, all six improved their industrial output, exports, savings and income per person. But the fairly optimistic tone of the report contrasts with its more gloomy analysis. In no single country did reform work unambiguously in the right way. Worse, these six countries had deteriorating rates of investment. Worth $1.6 billion in 1993, foreign direct investment is so negligible in Africa (it gets only 3% of global flows) that the study does not even measure it, let alone assess its rates of return. Only 13 of the countries studied even kept any data on private investment.

Ghana is the nearest the Bank can find to a model reformer. Its economy grew by an impressive 4% annually in 1988–92. But to achieve this, Ghana has been carefully nurtured by a Fund and Bank determined to ensure a success in Africa. Little private foreign investment has

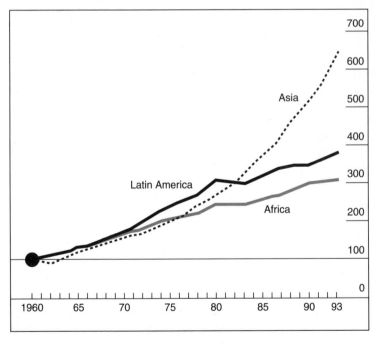

Figure A Index numbers of real GDP for different regions (1960 = 100)

Source: *The Economist,* 29 June 1996

followed, and it has gone into gold, not into manufacturing. Ghanaians are still among Africa's poorest people: GDP per person is $450. Ghana's national saving rate averaged 7.5% of GDP over 1987–91, compared with 33% for the fast-growing East Asian 'tiger' economies; its gross domestic investment rate is only 16% of GDP.

Those who disagree with the World Bank orthodoxy worry that Africa's economies are too fragile to withstand such demanding reforms. The chief economist at Oxfam argues that the high real interest rates required to meet short-term IMF monetary targets, coupled with the removal of import protection, kill off exactly the small industries that Africa needs to nurture. Untempered deregulation can undermine livelihoods of the poor, he argues, as it has for the farmers that Oxfam works with in eastern Zambia.

1. Contrast the economic performance of sub-Saharan Africa during recent years with that of other parts of the developing world.
[10 marks]
2. Explain why a lack of investment may be an important explanation of slow economic growth in sub-Saharan Africa. [10 marks]
3. Evaluate the economic policies which the passage suggests help to account for 'Africa's disastrous performance' in the 1980s.
[20 marks]
4. Evaluate the impact of structural adjustment policies in Africa.
[20 marks]

Chapter Five

Income distribution and development

'Despite its financial crisis, Mexico has achieved one economic distinction: it has the world's fastest growing number of billionaires with 13 in 1994. The combined wealth of these individuals is more than double the combined wealth of the poorest 17 million Mexicans, whose share of national income is falling.'   Oxfam, 1995

In Chapter 1, the focus of attention was on **absolute poverty**. In this chapter we shall be looking at the distribution of income within individual less-developed countries, and emphasizing the notion of **relative poverty** and inequality. The argument here is that poverty must be defined with respect to a **comparator group**.

An individual or a household may have more than enough income to sustain life, but the standard of living may still be very low compared with the average for the country as a whole, and that individual or household would thus still be regarded as 'poor'. As an economy grows – that is, as *per capita* incomes rise – so the income level defining poverty also rises. Relative poverty is thus specific with respect to both time and place.

The majority of poor countries are characterized by a variety of wide economic and social inequalities: inequalities in the distribution of income and wealth; between urban and rural areas; and between

---

Poverty as deprivation

'Poverty can be defined objectively and applied consistently only in terms of the concept of relative deprivation ... The term is understood objectively rather than subjectively. Individuals, families and groups in the population can be said to be in poverty when they lack the resources to obtain the types of diets, participate in the activities and have the living conditions and amenities which are customary, or are at least widely encouraged or approved, in the societies to which they belong. Their resources are so seriously below those commanded by the average individual or family that they are, in effect, excluded from ordinary living patterns, customs and activities.'

Source: Peter Townsend (a distinguished sociologist), 'Poverty and relative deprivation', in Wedderburn, D. (ed.), Poverty, Inequality and Class Structure, Cambridge University Press, 1974

---

different regions and ethnic or racial groups. Inequalities with respect to 'modern' sector facilities (employment, housing, education, health) are also significant.

Economists have focused their attention on the distribution of income, largely because even though the data are often incomplete and inaccurate, they are nevertheless available and are an indication of the wider inequalities referred to above.

The **size distribution of income** shows how many persons or households receive how much income, summarized in the **Lorenz curve** (see Figure 7). The 45-degree line, 0D, is the line of perfect equality, and the further away the actual Lorenz curve is from the 45-degree line, the greater is the degree of inequality in the size distribution of income. Hence Finland is less unequal than Brazil in the diagram.

The **Gini coefficient** is a measure of income distribution – the higher the ratio, the greater the degree of inequality. It is the ratio of the area

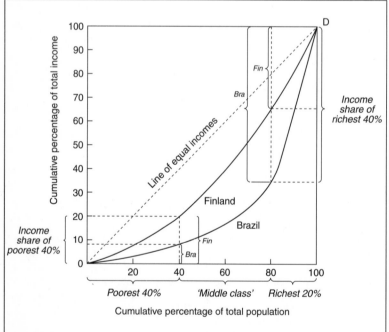

Figure 7 Lorenz curve: income distribution in Finland (1991) and Brazil (1989)

Source: UNDP, *Trade and Development Report 1997*

between the line of equal income and the Lorenz curve to the total area below the line. Table 5 on page 58 shows the Gini coefficient and the share in income or consumption of the lowest 20 per cent and highest 20 per cent of income recipients. As of the years to which the data relate, Sierra Leone had the highest Gini coefficient, closely followed by Brazil. Other countries with high Gini coefficients include Chile, Columbia, Guatemala, Kenya, Panama, Paraguay, South Africa and Zimbabwe.

In general, poor less-developed countries have higher levels of inequality than richer developed economies. The formerly centrally planned economies such as Hungary and Poland tended to have lower Gini coefficients.

However, in the 1990s inequality increased significantly, in the former centrally planned economies of eastern Europe and also in China. Greater inequality was also evident in the 1980s in Latin America. In many parts of Asia, levels of inequality have also been rising. With respect to Africa, it has been suggested (by UNDP, 1997) that there has been a process of 'equalizing downwards' across much of the personal income distribution as monetary sectors have contracted relative to subsistence sectors, real wages have fallen and the rural–urban gap has narrowed.

While a more equitable distribution of income may well be an objective of economic development, it also has a **functional value**. *This is because different income distributions will have varying impacts on the processes of growth and development in any given economy at any one time.* The distribution of income may well influence savings and investment, for example. The rich may save more than the poor, but their investments may be in non-productive assets – urban real-estate, foreign bank accounts, etc.

Income distribution also affects *patterns of consumption.* The rich may have a higher propensity to consume luxury, imported commodities, whereas the consumption of the poor will be dominated by essential items – basic foodstuffs, clothing and footwear, housing and household items (cooking utensils, basic furniture, etc.) – all produced locally and using unsophisticated, labour-intensive technologies.

Issues concerning income distribution are thus at the heart of the debate over *what* economic development should be about (**normative issues**) and *how* it can be achieved (**policy issues**).

Conclusions

Many economists argue that there is a conflict between **equity** and **efficiency**. This means that economies that emphasize greater equality –

Table 5 Distribution of income or consumption

Country	Year	Gini coefficient (%)	Share in income or consumption (%)	
			Lowest 20%	Highest 20%
Tanzania	1993	38.1	6.9	45.4
Zimbabwe	1990	56.8	4.0	62.3
Sierra Leone	1989	62.9	1.1	63.4
Nigeria	1992/3	45.0	4.0	49.4
Bangladesh	1992	28.3	9.4	37.9
Nepal	1995/6	36.7	7.6	44.8
India	1994	29.7	9.2	39.3
Pakistan	1991	31.2	8.4	39.7
China	1995	41.5	5.5	47.5
Indonesia	1995	34.2	8.4	43.1
Thailand	1992	46.2	5.6	52.7
Bolivia	1990	42.0	5.6	48.2
Jamaica	1991	41.1	5.8	47.5
Peru	1994	44.9	4.9	50.4
Egypt, Arab Rep.	1991	32.0	8.7	41.1
Russian Federation	1993	31.0	7.4	38.2
Brazil	1995	60.1	2.5	64.2
South Africa	1993	58.4	3.3	63.3
Hungary	1993	27.9	9.7	38.1
Poland	1992	27.2	9.3	36.6
Malaysia	1989	48.4	4.6	53.7
United Kingdom	1986	32.6	7.1	39.8
Switzerland	1982	36.1	7.4	43.5
Germany	1989	28.1	9.0	37.1

Source: World Bank, *World Development Report 1998/99*

through, for example, land reform, highly progressive taxation and an interventionist state – may as a result sacrifice economic growth. Put the other way round, *economies that wish to grow rapidly must accept greater inequality in the distribution of income.* Greater equality is thus seen as a 'luxury' that poor countries cannot afford, but which may be attainable once higher *per capita* incomes are achieved.

Economists have looked long and hard at the data on economic growth and income distribution. Most have concluded that there is no hard and fast relationship. The East Asian economies have grown rapidly with below-average levels of inequality (this is especially true of Taiwan – see Figure 8). Other economies emphasizing greater equality – for example Cuba – are experiencing severe economic difficulties, not least owing to the lack of material incentives and inadequate market mechanisms. China is now a rapidly growing economy and inequality is undoubtedly on the increase. Many sub-Saharan African economies are highly unequal and stagnant.

There is thus no simple economic model linking growth and equity. Inequality and poverty together condemn large numbers of people to malnutrition, poor housing, limited educational opportunities and

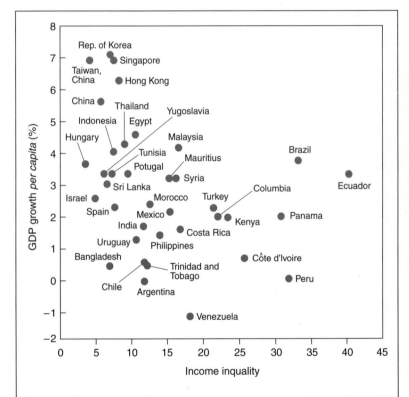

Figure 8 Income inequality* and the growth of GDP, 1965–89

Source: World Bank, 1991

*The ratio of the income shares of the richest 20 per cent and poorest 20 per cent of the population. Data on income distribution are from surveys conducted mainly in the late 1960s and early 1970s.

unemployment. A redistribution of income could raise the productivity and hence the output of such people by making them healthier, better educated and more active participants in the development process.

Progressive taxation might also curb excessive **conspicuous consumption** by the rich in poor countries, thus increasing saving and, it is hoped, productive investment.

KEY WORDS

Absolute poverty	Functional value
Relative poverty	Normative issues
Comparator group	Policy issues
Size distribution of income	Equity
Lorenz curve	Efficiency
Gini coefficient	Conspicuous consumption

Further reading

Lal, D., Chapter 5 in *The Poverty in 'Development Economics'*, 2nd edn, Institute of Economic Affairs, 1997.

Munday, S., Chapter 5 in *Markets and Market Failure*, Heinemann Educational, 2000.

Todaro, M., Chapter 5 in *Economic Development*, 5th edn, Longman, 1994.

United Nations Development Programme, *Trade and Development Report*, Oxford University Press, 1997.

Useful websites

AfricaNews Online: www.africanews.org
Asia-related news: www.asiawww.com/misc/news.htm
Asian Development Board: www.adb.org
Asian Recovery Information Centre of the ADB: http://aric.adb.org

Essay topics

1. Assess the relationship between the distribution of income in a country and that country's economic development.   [20 marks]
2. The path to economic development for the least developed economies is blocked by obstacles which the developed economies have not had to face or which they have already overcome.
   (a) Explain briefly the major obstacles to economic development faced by developing countries.   [10 marks]

(b) With the aid of examples, discuss whether these obstacles are best overcome by free market forces or government intervention.

[15 marks]

[OCR specimen paper, 2000]

Data response question

This task is based on a question set by Edexcel in a specimen paper in 2000. Read the article, and study Table A. Then answer the questions.

Living in poverty

In the 1970s, the then president of the World Bank, Robert McNamara, called world attention to the basic human needs of those in what he called 'absolute poverty'. He said that there will always be 'relative poverty' in the sense of income differentials between richer and poorer, but he wanted the World Bank to focus on those in 'absolute poverty – a condition of life so degraded by disease, illiteracy, malnutrition and squalor as to deny its victims basic human necessities'. The Bank then identified approximately the lowest 40 per cent of the population in developing countries as being in absolute poverty – about 900 million with an average per capita income of less than US$100 a year.

Two decades after McNamara's charge to the World Bank to attempt to reduce absolute poverty, the new president, Lewis Preston, still had to proclaim that 'no task should command higher priority for the world's policymakers than that of reducing global poverty'. In many countries, the gains from growth have not been reaching the poor. Why not?

The answers relate in part to:

* the rate of growth
* the pattern of growth
* the failure of government policies.

A slow rate of growth increases the total number of poverty for two reasons: there is not only a weak 'trickle down' effect, but even worse, when a country's growth is slow, its politicians need to gain political support. They then do so by in effect 'buying' support through the granting of favours such as foreign exchange allocations, import quotas, or subsidies. These rent-producing favours go to the non-poor: businessmen, large farmers, trade unions, and the army.

These inappropriate policies, in turn, tend to perpetuate a slow rate of growth. A vicious circle of slow growth and political favouritism then intensifies inequality and perpetuates poverty. A higher rate of growth is needed before politicians believe that they can afford to introduce policies that favour the poor.

The pattern of growth also matters in determining who are the beneficiaries of growth. The incidence of poverty can increase if the pattern of growth is urban biased, displaces unskilled labour, alters relative prices to the disadvantage of the poor, creates a gender gap, deteriorates child welfare, and erodes traditional entitlements that served as safety nets.

At the same time, governmental policies may be inadequate to lift some groups out of poverty. The major inadequacy is the lack of policies that create jobs. It can be argued that, when the market-price system does not provide full employment, government should not ignore remedial action. When public deficiencies in nutrition, poor health, and lack of education perpetuate low productivity, governmental policies should not ignore investment in human resources. When public expenditures must be necessarily limited, governments should not direct their expenditures to the non-poor to the neglect of those in poverty. These same strictures apply to foreign aid donors and international lending agencies such as regional development banks and the World Bank.

Table A Rural and urban poverty in the 1980s

Region/country	Percentage of total population in rural areas	Infant mortality (per thousand live births)		Access to safe water (percentage of population)	
		Rural	Urban	Rural	Urban
Sub-Saharan Africa					
Ivory Coast	57	121	70	10	30
Ghana	65	87	67	39	93
Kenya	80	59	57	21	61
Asia					
India	77	105	57	50	76
Indonesia	73	74	57	36	43
Philippines	60	55	42	54	49
Latin America					
Guatemala	59	85	65	26	89
Mexico	31	79	29	51	79
Peru	44	101	54	17	73

Source: World Bank, *World Development Report 1990,* OUP

1. With reference to the passage, distinguish between absolute poverty and relative poverty as these concepts apply to developing countries. [10 marks]
2. Evaluate the factors which account for poor people in developing countries deriving little benefit from economic growth. [20 marks]
3. Examine policies which governments in developing countries might adopt to increase the rate of economic growth. [20 marks]
4. Discuss why private capital flows might be a more effective way of promoting economic development than relying on official development flows. [10 marks]

Chapter Six

Population and environment

'*Population must not be treated as an optional extra when concerns of poverty alleviation and sustainable development are being negotiated. We need a truly integrated set of population, environment and development policies.*'   Dr Nafis Sadik, Secretary General of the International Conference on Population and Development, Cairo, 1994

The second half of the twentieth century witnessed a population explosion. From 1900 to 1950, the world's human population is estimated to have grown from 1.6 billion to 2.5 billion people. In October 1999 the United Nations estimated that the world's population had reached 6 billion people, 4.8 billion of whom live in poor countries. Hence the twentieth century experienced an approximately four-fold population increase, with the post-1950 period more than doubling the figure.

The main factor responsible for the increase has been the rapid increase in **population growth** in developing countries. Growth peaked at 2.5 per cent a year around 1970 and has subsequently slowly declined to just under 2 per cent. In the industrialized countries, the rate of growth of population in 1990 was 0.6 per cent a year.

Future growth of the global population is built into its present age structure. A very high proportion of the populations of developing countries is young. For example, in 1990, 45 per cent of the population of Africa and 37 per cent of the population of Latin America and South Asia were below the age of 15 (compared with 22 per cent for the industrialized economies). Whatever happens to female **fertility** – that is, the number of children women have – huge future increases in the population can be expected.

Current estimates put global population in the middle of the twenty-first century at anywhere between 7.1 billion and 11.9 billion people. Clearly poor countries will face massive problems in terms of employment, industrialization, technology choice and the environment in dealing with such increased numbers of people.

Population growth is caused by **birth rates** exceeding **death rates**. In LDCs, death rates have fallen more rapidly than birth rates, while the opposite has occurred in the developed economies. Death rates fall as a result of improvements in nutrition and material conditions and the spread of medical knowledge and treatment. Reduced **infant mortality** and increased longevity for those who survive childhood have contributed to the decline in the death rate, and this in turn is reflected in increased **life expectancy**.

A decline in death rates (especially infant mortality rates) is followed, with a lag, by a fall in birth rates. Almost all studies of the determinants of fertility indicate that as fewer babies under the age of one year die, this leads to a fall, with a lag, in the birth rate. Other determinants of fertility include female education, labour-force participation, the availability of family planning services, and the effects of improved economic well-being. The fall in birth rates following the fall in death rates is known as the **demographic transition**.

Country variations in population growth and total fertility are given in Table 6. Some countries have dramatically reduced population growth and fertility rates – China and Korea for example. In others, such as the Philippines, Kenya and Nigeria, population growth and fertility rates have remained high.

Economic consequences of population growth
Rapid population growth has a number of economic consequences:

- A high proportion of the population is aged 15 and under, increasing pressure on resources for health and education.
- **Dependency ratios** are high. The high number of non-earning family members per earner limits female participation in the labour force and may keep older children out of education, either to look after younger children and/or to work to supplement family income.
- There is rapid growth in the numbers of *working age*, leading to pressures on governments to increase employment opportunities.
- There is increased **urbanization**, reflecting both the growth of population in urban areas and the migration of people from rural to urban areas, which between 1950 and 1990 is estimated to have accounted for 50 per cent of urban population growth.
- Resources which could have been devoted to investment have to be used to provide social capital (e.g. schools and hospitals).

A number of LDCs – for example, Brazil and Malaysia – have achieved high *per capita* rates of growth of income in the face of high rates of growth of population. *It cannot therefore be argued in a simplistic manner that rapid population growth prevents or impedes economic growth and development.* The causes of poverty are to be found in the inequalities, both national and international, identified in other chapters in this book.

Table 6 Rate of growth of population and total fertility rate, selected countries, 1980 – 97

Country	Average annual growth rate of population (%)		Total fertility rate births per woman	
	1980–90	1990–97	1980	1996
China	1.5	1.1	2.5	1.9
India	2.1	1.8	5.0	3.1
Bangladesh	2.4	1.6	6.1	3.4
Sri Lanka	1.4	1.2	3.5	2.3
Indonesia	1.8	1.7	4.3	2.6
Malaysia	2.6	2.3	4.2	3.4
Philippines	2.6	2.3	4.8	3.6
Korea. Rep. of	1.2	1.0	2.6	1.7
Singapore	1.7	1.9	1.7	1.7
Egypt. Arab Rep.	2.5	2.0	5.1	3.3
Nigeria	3.0	2.9	6.9	5.4
Kenya	3.4	2.6	7.8	4.6
World	1.7w	1.5w	3.7w	2.8w
Low-income	2.4	2.1	5.6	4.1
Middle-income	1.6	1.3	3.2	2.3
Lower middle income	1.6	1.2	3.1	2.2
Upper middle income	1.9	1.5	3.8	2.6
Low and middle income	2.0	1.6	4.1	3.0
East Asia and Pacific	1.6	1.3	3.1	2.2
Europe and Central Asia	0.9	0.1	2.5	1.8
Latin America and Carib.	2.0	1.7	4.1	2.8
Middle East and N. Africa	3.0	2.5	6.1	4.0
South Asia	2.2	1.9	5.3	3.4
Sub-Saharan Africa	2.9	2.7	6.6	5.6
High-income	0.7	0.7	1.9	1.7

Note: Total fertility rate represents the number of children that would be born to a woman if she were to live to the end of her childbearing years and bear children at each age in accordance with prevailing age-specific fertility rates. w = weighted average.

Source: World Bank, *World Development Report 1998–99*

Action needed now to avert disaster

JOHN VIDAL

Today the world will gain another 230,000 people. Every day a city the size of Sunderland, every week another Birmingham, every month a London, and every year another Germany to feed, water, and clothe.

All but three in every 100 of the newcomers will be born in a country whose finances are stretched, whose cities are swelling, where millions go hungry, and where the water and food is often scarce.

Is it possible to provide for such a world? The answer is that "Biosphere 1" – earth – can provide the climatic stability, atmospheric composition, and biological productivity for many billions of people more than are expected to be living in the next century, but almost all the world's scientists and resource experts say we are wasting and polluting our resources in a way that threatens all life.

There is no reason why anyone should go hungry or thirsty.

The problem is poverty and inequality rather than technology, and distribution and politics more than production. There is more than enough food to go round: 30 years ago the global food supply represented 2,360 calories a day per person; today it is 2,740 calories and food supplies are expected to outstrip population growth for at least 10 more years.

But the population explosion is a developing world phenomenon, with 2bn people going hungry every day due to a combination of inequitable land distribution, soil erosion, lack of infrastructure, grinding poverty in cities, and people unable to buy food from the world market.

Food also depends on water, widely expected to be the most serious issue in the next century.

Lack of it is already limiting farming and industrial growth in large areas of three of the most populous countries, China, India, and Indonesia. Fourteen African states suffer water "stress" with 11 more expected to join them in the next 25 years. With population growth inevitable, if present consumption and climatic patterns continue, says the United Nations, two of every three people will have limited access to fresh water by 2025, with up to 2bn in acute shortage ...

The Guardian, 22 September 1999

Nevertheless, rapid population growth does make development more difficult for the reasons given above. The problem of poverty is not merely one of numbers of people; it also involves issues relating to quality of life and material well-being. Population and developmental issues are inseparable from one another.

Development and the environment

'*The protection of the environment is an essential part of development. Without adequate environmental protection, development is undermined; without development, resources will be inadequate for needed investments, and environmental protection will fail.*'
World Bank, 1992

Some environmental problems are linked to the lack of economic development. In many poor countries, problems associated with lack of clean water and inadequate sanitation, indoor air pollution from the burning of wood, straw and animal dung (so-called 'biomass fuels'), and many types of land degradation such as erosion, waterlogging and salinization, are the direct result of poverty.

Other problems are the result of, or are exacerbated by, the growth of economic pollution, deforestation caused by commercial logging, and the overuse of water – all resulting from economic expansion that fails to take account of the value of the environment. In these cases, environmental effects have to be built into the decision-making process.

Rapid population growth makes it more difficult to deal with many environmental problems, and poverty and environmental degradation mutually reinforce one another.

For example, poor farmers without access to sufficient land may cultivate erosion-prone hillsides and move into tropical forest areas where crop yields on cleared fields usually fall dramatically after a few years. The search for firewood leads to the loss of trees and ground cover.

Environmental economics

Many **environmental effects** are not directly reflected in prices and hence do not influence decisions based on the market.

Externalities are an important category of environmental effect. For example, a factory may discharge a toxic chemical into a river, killing fish and making the river dangerous or insanitary. This adversely affects users of the river, who thus suffer from an **external diseconomy**.

A *positive externality* or *external economy* is when the actions of one party have a beneficial effect on others and for which they do not pay.

Environmental economics argues that the environment can be seen as a form of capital which produces a flow of goods and services to humankind. The environment:

POVERTY AND THE ENVIRONMENT: EXPLODING THE MYTHS

New evidence challenges a number of entrenched assumptions about poverty – environment interactions.

Myth 1: Most environmental degradation is caused by the poor
Globally, most environmental degradation is caused by the non-poor as the poor's consumption levels are still low relative to the rich.

Myth 2: Poverty reduction necessarily leads to environmental degradation
Studies have failed to show a common pattern in the relationship between poverty and resource use. The linkages between poverty and the environment are complex and require context specific analysis – there is no simple causal relationship. There is sufficient evidence to show that the generalization that poverty reduction and concern for the environment are incompatible does not hold true.

Myth 3: Population growth necessarily leads to environmental degradation
Traditionally, increased population growth has been assumed to necessarily lead to environmental degradation. New evidence suggests there is no clear relationship. While initially degradation can occur as population increases, some times the resulting higher value of land, say, leads to better use of it, including conservation measures. Halting population growth or removing people from densely settled areas might improve neither productivity nor resource quality.

Myth 4: The poor are too poor to invest in the environment
The conventional wisdom has been that poor people are too impoverished to mobilize resources for enhancing the environment. In some cases this is true. However, numerous experiences now demonstrate that when incentives are favourable, even the poor can mobilize enormous resources, particularly labour.

Myth 5: Poor people lack the technical knowledge for resource management
It is often assumed that a lack of technical knowledge is a key constraint to poor people's management of natural resources. Indeed, when poor people move to areas with new ecological regimes, or when something happens to change the balance under which their old technology developed, a period of adjustment is required. However, poor people are often blamed for things that are not their fault. For example, shifting cultivation has been blamed for destroying the environment, yet in some circumstances it is the most sustainable agricultural practice. Also evidence is increasingly showing that poor people have an enormous store of what is sometimes termed indigenous technical knowledge, such as the use of medicinal plants, water harvesting structures, fishing sites, etc. but this knowledge is often undervalued or completely ignored. More research is needed to fully appreciate the logic of poor people's management practices.

Source: UNDP, 'Attacking poverty while protecting the environment towards win–win policy options', background technical note produced for the UNDP/EC poverty and environment initiative, July 1999

- is a source of raw materials and energy, some of which are renewable but others of which are finite;
- absorbs the waste products of human life through its air, soil and water;
- serves a variety of other functions to humankind, including life support, health and amenity.

The notion that the environment is a form of capital means that, if the services derived from it are not to be depleted, environmental assets must be maintained intact or renewed when used up or degraded. Some environmental assets *can* be renewed or restored after use – for example, forests and farmland. Other environmental assets (oil and minerals) can be *substituted* for by manufactured capital which generates an income stream: revenues generated from oil can be invested in financial assets or used to develop both physical and human capital. Some environmental resources are, however, irreplaceable once lost or degraded – wilderness ecology, virgin tropical forest.

The idea that we can replace environmental assets by replicating or compensating projects is at the heart of the notion of **sustainable development** (see Chapter 2) and depends on putting values on environmental functions.

- In theory, all environmental externalities can be given a price. This is the **'polluter pays' principle**. Once applied, prices and incentives can be fixed to encourage desirable behaviour towards the environment and to penalize its abuse.
- In practice, a market-based solution to environmental problems in LDCs would be extremely difficult to design and to enforce, and there is so far little evidence that Third World countries are prepared to adopt market solutions to environmental problems.

Conclusions

Population, the environment and development are intimately linked. In 1992, the World Bank estimated that as total population grew between then and 2030, global food production would have to *double*, industrial output and energy use *triple* worldwide and increase *five-fold* in developing countries. The Bank concluded:

> 'This growth brings with it the risk of appalling environmental damage. Alternatively, it could bring with it better environmental protection, cleaner air and water, and the virtual elimination of acute poverty. Policy choices will make the difference.'

The British government, as part of its strategy to meet the international development targets, has stated that 'there should be a current **national strategy for sustainable development** (NSSD) in the process of implementation in every country by 2005, so as to ensure that current trends in the losses of environmental resources are effectively reversed at both global and national levels by 2015'. NSSD processes are intended to integrate environmental issues into national planning and underline the argument that sustainable development is integral to poverty elimination. Important aspects of NSSD processes include:

- putting people at the centre, especially the poor;
- building partnerships at the local level;
- ensuring consistency and coherence between existing plans;
- effective implementation and proper monitoring and evaluation;
- building on strategic planning processes by developing elements missing in them;
- ensuring sustainability considerations are integrated at all levels.

Specific examples of such policies include: encouraging good governance; reform of economic policies to protect the environment; urging the private sector to integrate environmental concerns into their decision-making and to develop environmentally friendly private sector products (clean technology, energy-efficient technology, eco-tourism); assisting civil society to promote environmental awareness; and encouraging public participation and action on environmental issues.

KEY WORDS

Population growth	Dependency ratios
Fertility	Urbanization
Birth rates	Environmental effects
Death rates	Externalities
Infant mortality	External diseconomy
Life expectancy	Sustainable development
Demographic transition	'Polluter pays' principle

Further reading

Anderton, A., Unit 101 in *Economics*, 3rd edn, Causeway Press, 2000.

Burningham, D., and Davies, J., Chapters 2 and 4 in *Green Economics*, 2nd edn, Heinemann Educational, 1999.

DFID, *Environmental Sustainability and Eliminating Poverty*, consultation document, London, March 2000.

Munday, S., Chapter 8 in *Markets and Market Failure*, Heinemann Educational, 2000.

Useful websites

Friends of the Earth: www.foe.co.uk

World Health Organization: www.who.org

Essay topics

1. (a) Discuss the consequences of rapid population growth in a developing country. [10 marks]
   (b) Assess *three* policy measures the government of a developing country could take to reduce the growth of that country's population. [10 marks]
2. (a) Explain what is meant by 'sustainable development'. [8 marks]
   (b) Assess whether population growth will necessarily result in damage to the environment. [12 marks]

Data response question

This task is based on a question set by Edexcel in 1996. Study Tables A and B and then, using your knowledge of economics, answer the questions that follow.

Table A Indicators of living standards in selected countries

	Birth rate, 1992 (per 1000 population)	Death rate, 1992 (per 1000 population)	Life expectancy at birth, 1992 (years)	Primary pupil/teacher ratio 1991
Mozambique	45	21	44	55
Sierra Leone	48	22	43	34
Bangladesh	31	11	55	63
Poland	13	10	70	17
Hungary	12	14	69	12
Uruguay	17	10	72	22
Saudi Arabia	35	5	69	16
Sweden	14	11	78	6

Source: World Bank *World Development Report 1994*, OUP

Table B Economic data

	GNP per head, 1992 ($000)	GNP average annual growth, 1980–92	Average annual rate of inflation, 1980 – 92	Total external debt per head, 1992 ($000)
Mozambique	0.06	–3.6	38.0	0.299
Sierra Leone	0.16	–1.4	60.8	0.288
Bangladesh	0.22	1.8	9.1	0.115
Poland	1.91	0.1	67.9	1.257
Hungary	2.97	0.2	11.7	2.126
Uruguay	3.34	–1.0	66.2	1.695
Saudi Arabia	7.51	–3.3	–1.9	NA
Sweden	27.01	1.5	7.2	NA

NA: figures not available.

Source: World Bank *World Development Report 1994*, OUP

1. With reference to three of the developing countries, Mozambique, Sierra Leone and Bangladesh, what are the implications of the population data for the economies of these countries? [6 marks]
2. How might the data for Poland and Hungary illustrate the problems of such countries in becoming market economies?
[6 marks]
3. (a) Explain how the data might enable you to compare the standard of living of a citizen in Sweden with that of a citizen in one of the developing countries shown in the table. [7 marks]
(b) With reference to evidence other than that shown in the table, discuss why it is difficult to make a precise comparison of the standard of living between two such citizens. [6 marks]

Chapter Seven

Agricultural and industrial development

'For *the newly emerging countries of the post-war period,
industrialisation was seen as synonymous with development, and
development implied catching up with the advanced countries, using
basically the same means.*'   United Nations Industrial Development
Organization

According to the World Bank:

> '*Agriculture is the basic industry for the world's poorest
> countries, employing approximately 70–80 per cent of the
> labour force of low-income developing countries and
> accounting for roughly 35–40 per cent of GDP.*'

The share of agriculture in national income generally declines as *per
capita* incomes rise, for two reasons. First, people spend a decreasing
percentage of incomes on food as incomes rise and secondly, as farmers
increase the productivity of their land and labour, the share of a
country's resources required to grow food for the rest of the population
decreases.

Because of this relative decline in the importance of agriculture as *per
capita* incomes rise, industry has been perceived to be the **leading sector**
in development. Many countries have adopted negative policies
towards agriculture, with the emphasis on transferring investible
resources from the rural/agricultural to the urban/industrial sector.
*This view has now been revised and the transformation of the
agricultural sector is seen as both a cause and a consequence of
successful development.*

Links between agricultural and industrial development

The *agricultural sector* plays a strategic role in the development of the
industrial sector:

- The agricultural sector provides a major market for manufactured
  goods, both inputs required for the transformation of agriculture
  (pumps for agricultural irrigation systems, implements, chemical
  fertilisers) and consumer goods (bicycles, radios, household utensils,
  cigarettes) which farmers increasingly demand as their incomes rise.
- Agriculture satisfies the food requirements of the urban population
  (if it does not, either prices and/or imports of foodstuffs rise).

- Agriculture releases labour and capital for the industrial sector. Labour migrates to the urban/industrial sector and savings are extracted in various ways – through taxation and voluntary saving, for example, or through forced extraction (as was the case in the former Soviet Union).
- Agricultural exports earn the foreign exchange required for the importation of machinery and equipment and intermediate inputs (for example, oil, chemicals) required for development.
- Agriculture provides many of the industrial sector's inputs – cotton, sisal, tobacco.

The *industrial sector* in turn supports agriculture:

- Industry provides the inputs required for agricultural modernization (tractors, fertilizers).
- Industry provides a market for a part of agricultural output through the processing and manufacture of foodstuffs for both domestic consumption and exports.

The contributions that agriculture can make to development illustrate some difficult choices that governments have to make when defining development policies and objectives. First, high prices may persuade farmers to produce and sell more, but low food prices benefit urban consumers and minimize inflationary pressures. Secondly, promotion of export crops increases foreign exchange earnings, but this might be at the expense of producing foodstuffs for the domestic market. Thirdly, taxation of the agricultural sector may be necessary to raise revenue to finance government expenditure, but higher taxes may act as a disincentive to farmers who may produce less and/or consume more of what they produce.

The distribution of world manufacturing value-added

Manufacturing value-added (MVA) is the difference between the value of output and the value of raw materials and intermediate inputs. It thus measures the value of factor services – wages, profits, interest and rent.

Table 7 gives data on the distribution of MVA for the period 1980–96, in both constant (1990) prices and current prices. Note that owing to variations in official exchange rates, the world distribution of MVA may change significantly depending on the choice of base year.

The main points of the table are:

- the collapse in the share of eastern Europe and the former USSR (more dramatic in constant than current prices);

Table 7 Distribution of world MVA, 1980–98

| | Industrialized countries | | | | | | Developing countries | | | | | | | | |
| | | | | | | | Regional groups | | | | Development groups | | | | |
Year	Eastern Europe and former USSR	Western Europe EU*	Western Europe Other	Japan	North America	Others	Latin America	Africa	South and East Asia	West Asia and Europe	NICs	Second-generation NICs	Least-developed countries	China	Others
Percentage share in world total MVA (at constant 1990 prices)															
1980	9.3	34.8	1.7	13.9	23.8	2.1	8.7	0.9	5.1	1.7	8.3	1.6	0.4	1.4	2.7
1985	9.6	22.2	1.5	15.7	23.7	1.9	5.9	1.0	6.5	2.0	8.3	1.8	0.4	2.0	2.9
1990	8.4	31.4	1.4	17.1	23.1	1.8	5.3	1.0	8.7	1.8	8.7	2.4	0.3	2.6	2.8
1994	3.8	31.4	1.5	15.4	24.4	1.9	5.7	0.9	12.4	1.8	9.5	2.8	0.3	4.8	3.0
1995	3.8	30.6	1.4	18.5	24.7	1.9	5.4	0.9	13.1	1.7	9.4	3.1	0.3	5.2	3.0
1996	3.6	29.8	1.4	17.0	24.4	1.8	5.5	0.9	13.9	1.7	9.7	3.1	0.3	5.5	3.0
1997†	3.5	29.5	1.4	16.7	24.6	1.8	5.5	0.9	14.2	1.8	9.8	3.4	0.3	5.9	3.0
1998‡	3.4	30.2	1.4	15.3	25.3	1.7	5.5	1.0	14.2	1.8	9.7	3.5	0.4	6.4	3.1
Percentage share in world total MVA (at current prices)															
1994	3.1	29.2	1.4	21.0	24.1	1.7	6.1	0.7	11.2	1.5	8.7	9.5	0.3	3.7	2.9
1995	2.9	29.8	1.5	20.9	22.8	1.7	5.9	0.8	12.1	1.6	9.1	9.4	0.4	4.3	2.9
1996	2.9	29.8	1.4	18.5	23.3	1.8	6.4	0.8	13.5	1.6	9.5	9.9	0.4	5.1	3.2
1997†	2.9	28.4	1.3	11.0	24.3	1.8	7.1	0.9	14.0	1.7	9.3	10.5	0.4	5.6	3.5

*Beginning of 1992, including estimates for the eastern part of Germany. † Provisional. ‡ Estimate.

NICs are Mexico, Yugoslavia (former), Hong Kong (China), Taiwan Province (China), India, Republic of Korea, Singapore.

Second-generation NICs are Morocco, Tunisia, Chile, Turkey, Indonesia, Malaysia, Philippines, Thailand.

Source: UNIDO, International Yearbook of Industrial Statistics 2000

- the virtually unchanged share, in both constant and current prices, of Japan and North America;
- a rise in the share of developing countries in world MVA from 16.4 per cent in 1994 to 23.4 per cent in 1997 (in current prices) and from 14.4 per cent in 1980 to 22.7 per cent in 1998 (in constant prices);
- in constant prices, the decline in the share of Latin America and the Caribbean and the more than doubling in the share of South and East Asia;
- the low and unchanging share of Africa in World MVA.

Note that these estimates exclude the People's Republic of China. Separate estimates put the latter's share of world MVA at 5.7 per cent in constant 1990 prices in 1996 (as compared to 2.0 per cent in 1985). Even though developing economies have increased their share of world MVA, they are still relatively marginal in aggregate as far as the world economy is concerned. In certain branches (for example, textiles, leather products and footwear) their share is higher.

Structural change

As noted above, as *per capita* incomes grow, there is a consistent decline in the share of the agricultural sector in national output, and a consistent increase in the share of the industrial sector.

The third major sector – *services* – has a less consistent pattern, although in higher income economies the service sector grows at the expense of the industrial sector.

Table 8 presents data on sectoral shares of GDP for 1980 and 1997. It can be seen that in 1997, almost one third of value-added originated in the agricultural sector in low-income economies, with South Asia and sub-Saharan Africa having the largest shares. Even in 1980, the manufacturing sector was relatively more important in East Asia and the Pacific than it was in the high-income economies. In sub-Saharan Africa, **structural change** has been very slow, reflecting stagnation and decline in many sub-Saharan economies.

Note that it is difficult to categorize accurately activities in the services sector. In the developed market economies there has been a marked shift into financial services and leisure activities.

In low-income economies, on the other hand, many people are occupied in a wide variety of low-productivity, low-income activities in the informal sector (such as petty traders, street hawkers, shoeshiners, barbers and in various illegitimate activities such as drug pushing, smuggling, prostitution, petty theft, and so on).

The sectoral distribution of the labour force changes less

Table 8 Structure of output (value-added as percentage of GDP)

Country group	Agriculture		Industry		Manufacturing		Services	
	1980	1997	1980	1997	1980	1997	1980	1990
Low-income	35	31	26	27	15	16	38	42
Middle-income	15	12	45	38	–	–	40	50
Lower middle-income	18	14	45	40	–	–	37	46
Upper middle-income	9	10	46	34	23	–	45	56
Low- and middle-income	18	16	42	36	22	–	40	48
East Asia and Pacific	28	19	44	45	32	33	28	36
Europe and Central Asia	–	11	–	36	–	–	–	53
Latin America and Carib.	10	10	40	33	27	21	50	57
Middle East and N. Africa	12	–	48	–	9	–	40	–
South Asia	38	27	25	28	17	18	37	44
Sub-Saharan Africa	22	25	36	30	14	16	42	45
High-income	3	–	36	–	24	–	61	–

Source: World Bank, 1999

dramatically, although employment data are less comprehensive and reliable.

Table 9 illustrates the distribution of MVA and population among selected groups of developing countries. Points to note include:

- the huge imbalance between the share of low-income economies in MVA in both constant and current prices and their share of developing country population;
- a similar imbalance with respect to the least-developed country category and the share of Africa (most least-developed economies are in sub-Saharan Africa);
- the fall in the relative share of Latin America in developing-economy MVA and the increase in the relative share of South and East Asia (in effect, the shift from strategies of import-substituting industrialization (ISI) to export-oriented industrialization (EOI) – see below).

For all groups of LDCs, the industrial sector's share of the total labour force is less than its share of national output. This is a reflection both of the concentration of underemployed, low-productivity labour in the agricultural sector, and of the general use of capital-intensive methods of production in the 'modern' industrial sector.

Table 9 Distribution of MVA and population among selected groups of developing countries (percentages)

Country group	MVA at constant 1990 prices						MVA at current prices				Population			
	1980	1985	1990	1995	1996	1997†	1994	1995	1996	1997†	1980	1985	1990	1997
Low-income	14.6	16.0	18.4	18.7	18.8	18.4	18.0	18.2	18.2	17.4	46.6	47.2	47.8	48.8
Middle-income	15.8	18.9	20.9	20.4	20.2	20.3	20.7	21.5	20.6	19.5	11.0	11.2	11.4	11.7
High-income	58.6	51.9	45.1	38.5	35.4	35.0	42.4	39.1	38.4	39.5	11.7	11.9	11.9	11.8
Developing countries	100.0	100.0	100.0	100.0	100.0	100.0	100.0	100.0	100.0	100.0	100.0	100.0	100.0	100.0
Least-developed countries	2.5	2.5	2.1	1.7	1.6	1.6	1.7	1.7	1.7	1.8	11.5	11.7	12.1	12.8
NICs	57.7	53.9	51.6	44.5	43.9	43.7	48.7	46.2	44.6	44.5	31.0	31.0	30.8	30.7
Second-generation NICS	10.8	11.8	14.3	15.2	15.3	15.2	15.9	16.5	16.7	15.5	11.2	11.3	11.2	11.2
Other developing countries	18.9	18.6	16.4	14.0	13.6	13.2	14.8	14.4	14.2	14.6	15.6	16.3	17.0	17.8
Developing countries	100.0	100.0	100.0	100.0	100.0	100.0	100.0	100.0	100.0	100.0	100.0	100.0	100.0	100.0
Africa	5.1	6.6	5.8	4.4	4.2	4.2	3.8	3.8	3.8	3.8	12.6	14.1	14.7	15.6
Latin America	46.6	38.1	31.5	25.6	24.5	24.7	31.4	29.1	23.6	29.9	11.3	11.2	11.2	11.2
South and East Asia	36.3	42.8	51.7	62.2	53.1	53.3	57.3	59.5	50.5	59.2	71.5	70.2	70.2	65.2
West Asia and Europe	12.0	12.7	11.0	7.8	7.8	7.8	7.5	7.5	7.1	7.1	3.6	3.9	3.9	4.0
Developing countries	100.0	100.0	100.0	100.0	100.0	100.0	100.0	100.0	100.0	100.0	100.0	100.0	100.0	100.0

† Provisional.

Source: *UNIDO, International Yearbook of Industrial Statistics, 2000*

Strategies of industrialization

As noted above, the LDCs have gradually increased their share of global MVA over the past two decades. The experience of industrialization in the Third World is highly uneven, however. Although the large Latin American economies remain the most industrialized in absolute terms, the most rapidly industrializing economies are located in East and South East Asia. In the mid-1990s – that is, before the Asian financial crisis – Republic of Korea, Brazil, China, Argentina and Taiwan were all in the 'world top 15' measured by MVA (accounting for just over 10 per cent of global MVA). With respect to trade in manufactured goods, Hong Kong, Republic of Korea and Taiwan were in the 'top 15' exporters together accounting for nearly 14 per cent of the global total.

Import-substituting industrialization

Import-substituting industrialization (ISI) is a strategy based on the domestic production of goods that were previously imported. It was initiated in many Latin American economies as a response to two world wars, and the intervening global depression when either imports were not available or there was insufficient foreign exchange to pay for them.

After the ending of World War II in 1945, and with the achievement of political independence for former colonies, many countries adopted ISI strategies (for example, India, Pakistan, Indonesia, and in the 1960s countries such as Nigeria, Kenya and Ghana). Typically the strategy involved the imposition of **tariffs** and other controls on imports to provide a protected domestic market for either domestic enterprises or the affiliates of transnational corporations (TNCs).

The process began with the domestic production of *consumer goods* such as shoes, and the importation of *investment goods* such as shoe-making machines and *intermediate goods* (leather, plastics, etc.). In theory, once consumer goods have been substituted, the next 'round' of ISI would concentrate on machinery and equipment (investment goods) and finally on to *capital goods* (machines that can make other machines).

These expectations were not realized in practice. In the early 1960s, for example, Brazil appeared to have 'exhausted' the consumer goods stage of ISI without moving smoothly into the next stage. Economic growth slowed, inflation accelerated and social unrest grew. The Brazilian military staged a coup in 1964. This experience was not unique to Brazil but was repeated in many other countries – Argentina, Pakistan, Indonesia, Nigeria to name a few. *It was concluded that ISI had failed as an industrialization strategy.*

The *orthodox* explanation for the apparent failure was that there had been too much government intervention in the market mechanism (see 'Alternative theoretical perspectives on development' in Chapter 3). In particular, high tariff levels and overvalued exchange rates had discriminated against these countries' exports (for many the major export sector was agriculture) and had led to the creation of a high-cost, inefficient, uncompetitive domestic manufacturing sector.

Structuralist explanations focused on a variety of factors:

- continued shortage of foreign exchange – the balance-of-payments constraint on development;
- the dependence on foreign technology – considered 'inappropriate' to the resources and needs of LDCs;
- the inability of ISI to break or relax the various structural constraints or bottlenecks characteristic of the LDC economy.

Export-oriented industrialization

At the same time that ISI appeared to be breaking down, a number of East and South East Asian economies – Singapore, Hong Kong, South Korea and Taiwan – were emerging as increasingly important exporters of manufactured goods.

The **export-oriented industrialization** (EOI) strategies of these economies were based upon:

- outward-oriented trade policies that provided incentives favouring neither the domestic market nor the export market (neutrality);
- the use of labour-intensive technologies in the manufacturing sector, consistent with factor endowments and comparative advantage;
- reliance on the market for a more efficient allocation of resources;
- minimal government intervention.

That these economies have been very successful is not open to doubt. The original four economies have been joined by a number of other newly industrializing economies (NIEs) – Malaysia, Thailand, Indonesia and China – in what has become the most dynamic and rapidly growing region in the world, the Asia–Pacific region.

However, economists argue over how these economies have succeeded. The orthodox explanation is trade. The critics of this view emphasize the important role that the state has played in the economic life in all these countries, most notably in Taiwan and South Korea.

SOUTH KOREA

The American economist Alice Amsden, in her book Asia's Next Giant: South Korea and Late Industrialisation (Oxford University Press, 1989), emphasized the strategic role of the Korean state in what she called **late industrialization**. She argued, somewhat provocatively, that the state had deliberately got prices 'wrong' – for example, subsidized credit provided to sectors considered important by the government – in order to achieve its development objectives.

Apart from the interventionist state, the major agent of expansion in late industrialization was in the modern industrial enterprise. In Korea, this was the chaebol, a large diversified business group which had penetrated the lower end of numerous foreign markets and had supplanted the need for foreign firms to undertake investments in targeted industries. (Amsden argued that Korea had depended heavily on foreign loans but that there had been relatively little direct foreign investment, except in a number of relatively labour-intensive sectors.)

The chaebol themselves increasingly invested overseas, with Samsung, Daewoo, Hyundai and LG (formerly Lucky Goldstar) leading the way (Financial Times, 10 February 1995).

Amsden and other writers on South Korea emphasized the role of the developmental state, the growth of indigenous capital and the possibilities for capitalist development in so-called 'peripheral countries'. The shift by South Korea in the 1970s into heavy industries (engineering, shipbuilding, industrial chemicals, automobiles) and the increasing innovative capabilities of the chaebol (based on increasing research and development expenditures and a commitment to education, especially technical and scientific) provided support to those who argued that the notion of dependency was static and ahistorical, and that independent industrialization was possible in the Third World.

Conclusions

The record of industrialization in the Third World is mixed. When successful, industrialization transforms the structure of the economy and leads to sustained economic growth. To be successful, however, industrialization requires a stable macroeconomic environment and the simultaneous promotion of agricultural development.

The lessons from the East Asian experience seem to be the following:

- Direct but selective government intervention is needed, both to create new productive capacity and to ensure that existing capacity is used efficiently.
- There has to be investment in human capital formation, with special emphasis on scientific and technical education and training.

- There has to be investment in research and development (R&D) activities.
- Finally, appropriate institutions have to be created to overcome specific market failures that inhibit industrial development – quality, assurance, training, information collection, technology diffusion, testing and research support institutes.

KEY WORDS

Leading sector	Tariffs
Structural change	Export-oriented
Import-substituting	industrialization
industrialization	Late industrialization

Further reading

Grant, S., Chapter 2 in *Economic Growth and Business Cycles*, Heinemann Educational, 1999.

Lipsey, R., and Chrystal, K., Chapter 33 in *Principles of Economics*, 9th edn, Oxford University Press, 1999.

Sloman, J., Chapter 25 in *Economics*, 4th edn, Prentice Hall, 1999.

Todaro, M., Chapters 8 and 9 in *Economic Development*, 5th edn, Longman, 1994.

Useful websites

One World: www.oneworld.org

United Nations Industrial Development Organisation: www.unido.org

Essay topics

1. Developing countries frequently depend heavily upon primary production.
   (a) Explain what is meant by primary production and the problems caused by this dependency. [10 marks]
   (b) Discuss the difficulties faced by developing countries when they try to diversify their production. [15 marks]
   [OCR specimen paper, 2000]

2. (a) Explain *two* policies which result from the economic structure of developing countries. [8 marks]
   (b) Identify and evaluate alternative policies to overcome these problems. [12 marks]
   [UCLES, June 1997]

Data response question

This task is based on a question set by UCLES in 1998. Read the article and study Figure A and Table A, and then answer all the questions.

The changing nature of agriculture in Kenya

All over Kenya, farmers have switched from growing potatoes, carrots, maize and cabbages, which local people eat, to the production of flowers or luxury vegetables like French beans, which are flown to Europe.

Now they can pay school fees for most of their children, replace their thatched huts with corrugated-iron-roofed houses and have piped water in their homes. The only problem is that food prices are doubling every two years. Maize, which many of them once grew, now has to be trucked in from 200 kilometres away.

Horticulture has overtaken coffee and become the country's second export commodity after tea. By 1992, Kenya was shipping out 57,000 tons of flowers and luxury vegetables, from which it earned 78 million US dollars per year. By the turn of the century, horticulture is expected to bring in 406 million US dollars per year. Among horticultural products, flowers are the biggest earner. Multinational food companies – such as Britain's Brooke Bond and the US's Del Monte – pioneered the export-oriented production.

In 1991, the army bulldozed 100 acres of tropical forest to make way for Sian Roses. Large quantities of water from Lake Naivasha, the only fresh-water lake in the Rift valley, are pumped to the precious export crop. Ecologists fear that the lake will dry up and warn that massive amounts of dangerous pesticides and fertilisers are draining into it from the rose plantations.

Table A Exports of cut flowers from Kenya, 1980–91

Year	Cut flower exports (tons)	Value of cut flowers (K£000)
1980	3 788	4 924
1991	16 405	49 215

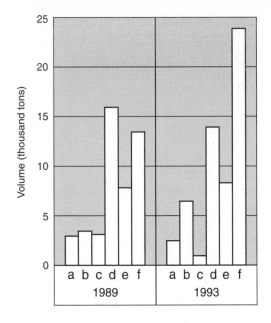

Key

(a) mangoes

(b) avocados

(c) pineapples

(d) French beans

(e) Asian vegetables

(f) cut flowers

Figure A Export commodities by volume, 1989–93

1. (a) Use Figure A to identify which export had the greatest rate of
   (i) growth and (ii) decline between 1989 and 1993.   [2 marks]
   (b) Using the information in Table A, explain what happened to the
   average price of exported cut flowers between 1980 and 1991.
   Justify your answer.   [2 marks]
   (c) In what ways is Kenya's pattern of trade typical of many
   developing countries?   [2 marks]
2. (a) To what extent might the principle of comparative advantage
   explain the production of flowers in Kenya for sale in western
   Europe?   [4 marks]
   (b) State and explain *one* favourable and *one* unfavourable effect of
   the growth of the flower industry on Kenya's balance of payments.
   [4 marks]
3. Discuss how the level of welfare in Kenya might change as a result
   of the agricultural developments referred to in the article.[6 marks]

Chapter Eight

International trade and economic development

'*TRADE, NOT AID*' A popular development slogan

Does trade lead to development?

The poor countries are **open economies** with imports and exports accounting for a large proportion of national output.

Output and employment levels and rates of growth are highly dependent on export performance. Imports of machinery and equipment, fuels and raw materials are essential inputs for the development process.

During the colonial period the colonies were a captive market for the manufactured goods of the metropolitan powers, while in return supplying raw materials and tropical foodstuffs. For the poorest countries, in particular, *these patterns of trade have changed only slowly.* Given the specific problems of those countries dependent on **primary commodity exports,** it is not surprising that the system of international trade is sometimes seen to be inherently unfair to the poorer countries.

Orthodox trade theory – the theory of **comparative advantage** – predicts that all countries can benefit by specializing in the production and trade of those commodities in which they have the lowest relative production costs; differences in comparative costs are based on inter-country differences in factory endowments. Poor countries with an abundance of labour and a scarcity of capital should specialize in the production and export of *labour-intensive* commodities, while rich countries with plentiful capital and scarce labour should specialize in *capital-intensive* commodities.

LDC trade

The sterotypical picture of trade is of LDCs exporting primary products (agricultural and mineral products) to the industrial economies in return for manufactured goods. *In practice, developed economies export significant quantities of primary products (especially temperate foodstuffs) and the LDCs export manufactured goods.*

Table 10 gives an overview of rates of growth of trade for the non-oil

Table 10 Trade of non-oil-exporting developing countries, 1970–96 (average annual percentage increase in value)

	1970–79		1982–88		1989–96	
	Exports	Imports	Exports	Imports	Exports	Imports
All non-oil exporters†	21.4	17.5	8.8	4.8	11.7	13.5
of which:						
Sub-Saharan Africa	14.0	13.4	3.2	1.0	6.2	6.1
Latin America	18.8	15.0	2.9	−1.9	9.7	13.9
Asia	26.8	21.3	13.0	9.1	12.7	14.1
Memo items:						
All developing countries	22.0	18.6	2.0	2.6	11.7	12.4
of which:						
China	25.7	28.2	12.3	16.4	15.9	12.8

*Excluding 1974 and 1975. † excluding China.

Source: UNCTAD database

LDCs over the period 1970–96. It can be seen that for all regions, the rapid growth of trade which characterized the 1970s fell dramatically in the 1980s, even though as in the case of Asia exports were still growing rapidly. The late-1980s to mid-1990s saw a marked recovery in export growth for all regions except Asia. The recovery in the growth of imports, particularly in the case of Africa and Latin America, is in part attributable to policies of trade liberalization in those countries, often a part of stabilization and structural adjustment programmes (see Chapter 4).

High rates of growth of exports can be offset by equally high or even higher rates of growth of imports, and for the great majority of low-income economies trade deficits grew in the 1990s. Where countries have managed to maintain high rates of economic growth, the majority have experienced a deterioration in their trade balance financed by inflows of private capital, often short-term. With a loss of confidence, inflows quickly become outflows (as in the Asian financial crisis in 1997) and are followed by economic contraction and import cuts.

It is difficult to know why trade deficits have been growing so rapidly in LDCs. UNCTAD (1999) suggests it is the result of declining terms of trade (see below), slow growth in the industrial countries, and the 'big bang' liberalization of trade and capital account transactions. Many LDCs remain dependent on a small number of types of export. For example:

- tobacco and gold account for over 40 per cent of Zimbabwe's exports;
- coffee and petroleum account for 37 per cent of Colombia's exports;
- bauxite and alumina account for 52 per cent of Jamaica's exports.

However, two examples can be given of the changes that have occurred:

- *Bangladesh*: In 1972, jute products accounted for 90 per cent of total exports; by 1991, the share of jute had fallen to 18 per cent and ready-made garments accounted for over 50 per cent of the total.
- *Mauritius*: In 1976, sugar accounted for 72 per cent of total exports; by 1991, sugar's share had fallen to 29 per cent and clothing and textiles accounted for 55 per cent of the total.

LDCs continue to dominate world trade in certain commodities – petroleum, sugar, coffee, copper, rubber, tin, tea, palm oil, bananas – but this dominance/dependence can be seen as a weakness rather than as a strength. As can be seen in Figure 9, primary commodity prices

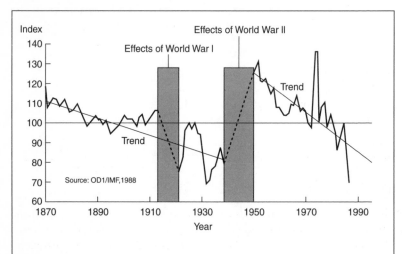

Figure 9 Real commodity prices deflated by price of manufactures, 1870–1986 (1980 = 100)

Source: ODI/IMF, 1988

appear to be prone to a long-term decline relative to other prices, and instability – fluctuations around the trend –increased in the 1980s (see Figure 9).

There has been a remarkable changes in the composition of developing countries' exports, with manufactures already accounting for almost 57 per cent of total exports by 1989. But many developing countries, especially the least-developed ones, remain heavily dependent on primary-commodity exports (especially tropical beverages, agricultural raw materials and minerals, ore and metals). Since 1980, the markets for these commodities have remained depressed, despite some short-term rises in prices in these unstable markets. In addition the majority of international commodity agreements have fallen into disarray. Attempts at diversification by the smaller, poorer, primary-commodity exporting economies have typically not been successful, and even after the completion of the **Uruguay Round** and the establishment of the **World Trade Organization** (WTO), barriers to trade are still significant.

Terms of trade

Terms of trade refers to the value of one bundle of commodities in terms of another. In developing economies, attention has been focused on the behaviour of **net barter terms of trade** (NBTT). An NBTT is a price index of exports divided by a price index of imports, expressed as a percentage:

$$\text{Net barter terms of trade} = (P_E/P_I) \times 100.$$

If the price of exports is falling relative to the price of imports (or if the price of exports is raising less rapidly than the price of imports) then the NBTT is deteriorating; that is, a given bundle of exports buys a smaller bundle of imports.

Many economists have argued that the NBTTs of primary-commodity exporters show a long-run (secular) tendency to deteriorate. Various reasons have been put forward as to why this should be the case:

- In the developed industrialized economies, powerful trades unions are able to capture the benefits of productivity gains in the form of higher wages; whereas in LDCs, higher productivity in the primary commodity sector leads to lower prices.
- Income elasticities of demand for agricultural producers decline as income rises, so that demand for them grows more slowly than demand for manufactured goods.

THE WORLD TRADE ORGANIZATION

On 1 January 1995, a comprehensive round of multilateral trade agreements embodying the results of the Uruguay Round of Multilateral Trade Negotiations was concluded, and the World Trade Organization (WTO) was formed. Out of the present 135 members of the WTO, some 98 are from the developing world.

As LDCs seek to extend their market access, the WTO framework will increasingly influence their integration into the global economy, as well as set the boundaries for their trade and investment relations with the rest of the world. The WTO will have an influence on regional trade policy which, in turn, will have profound economic and social implications for national economies.

The effects will be all the more profound because trade liberalization is no longer confined to reducing barriers to trade but includes much broader issues like rules governing foreign direct investment, technology patents, intellectual property rights, labour and environmental standards in production. They will thus have widespread effects in other areas of domestic policy.

The trade-related investment provisions and the trade-related intellectual property rights in particular will have important implications for development. The phasing out of the Multi Fibre Agreement by 2005 will also have a differential effect on the major exporters of textiles and garments.

The WTO, an inter-governmental institution, has been criticized for failing to reflect the interests of the developing countries. It is argued that the balance of rights and obligations in the multilateral trading system, as embodied in the WTO, favours the developed countries. Developing-country governments want to ensure that the WTO agenda reflects the balance of interests of the developed and developing economies.

In light of this and the increasing importance of the WTO, it is argued that the LDCs must participate more effectively in the entire spectrum of the WTO negotiation process.

- Technological advances have led to the development of synthetic substitutes for many primary commodities such as, plastics substituted for rubber, synthetic fibres substituted for cotton and wool.
- Technological changes have reduced the weight of metal and other minerals required to produce a unit of manufactured goods. There has also been a change in the composition of manufactured output, away from heavy industries (e.g. iron and steel, shipbuilding) towards newer activities less dependent on raw materials (e.g. electronics).
- The protection of agricultural sectors in the developed economies has created exportable surpluses of some agricultural commodities and reduced import demands for others. For example, sugar beet has been produced at the expense of sugar cane imports.

These are all convincing arguments supporting the hypothesis, but the empirical evidence has not always provided unambiguous support. Much depends on the time period covered and the country and commodity coverage.

There have been short periods, in 1973–76 and 1979–81, when the NBTTs moved in favour of primary producers, but there were longer periods in which changes in NBTTs favoured the developed economies.

The data in Table 11 indicate that developing countries as a whole (including oil exporters and China) experienced a sharp drop in their terms of trade from 1982 to 1988 by more than 5 per cent a year. Export volumes rose by a slightly smaller amount and the purchasing power of exports thus fell by over 1 per cent a year. In the subsequent period (1989–96) the terms of trade stabilized and the volume and purchasing power of exports rose. This recovery was short-lived, however, and oil and non-oil primary-commodity prices fell spectacularly from the end of1996 to the beginning of 1999 (the impact of the Asian financial crisis).

If we consider non-oil exporters, however, we see a different picture in the 1989–96 period. The terms of trade continued to fall in the latter period, although strong export volume growth resulted in growing purchasing power of exports. (Note that declining terms of trade still led to income losses, even when the purchasing power of exports was growing.)

More recent work by both the IMF and the World Bank seems to provide statistical evidence in support of the 'Prebisch–Singer hypothesis'. There is evidence of a statistically significant downward trend in the net barter terms of trade for the period since 1900.

Table 11 Export volume, purchasing power of exports and terms of trade of developing countries, 1982–96 (average annual percentage change)

	1982–88	*1989–96*
All developing countries		
Export volume	4.7	8.2
Terms of trade	–5.4	0.2
Purchasing power of exports	–1.4	8.3
Non-oil-exporters		
Export volume	8.6	11.6
Terms of trade	–1.3	–1.5
Purchasing power of exports	7.2	9.9

Source: UNCTAD, *Handbook of International Trade and Development Statistics*, various issues.

Short-run earnings instability

It has been argued that the prices of primary commodities are more unstable in the short run than those of manufactured goods. This, in turn, gives rise to short-run **instability** of export earnings, which are quite damaging to the growth and development prospects of primary commodity exporters.

Most, though not all, poor countries are **price-takers** on the world markets for their exports. That is, the production of primary commodity exports in individual countries is generally small in relation to international production. The price instability of primary commodities is attributable to:

- the competitive nature of world commodity markets;
- the relatively inelastic price elasticities of supply and demand, with shifts in the supply or demand curves requiring large price changes to restore market equilibrium;
- the vulnerability of agriculture to adverse weather conditions;
- fluctuations in demand in the industrial countries for primary commodities;
- the agricultural policies of the industrial countries restricting market access and – through the use of quotas and controlled prices – reducing the size of the 'free' market.

International commodity agreements

Large fluctuations in the export earnings of developing countries may be caused by:

- excessive variability of supply and demand;
- low price elasticity of supply and demand;
- excessive specialization on one or two commodities;
- the concentration of exports in particular markets.

The empirical evidence on export-earning instability is inconclusive and does not suggest that developing countries as a group suffer extreme instability as a result of their dependence on primary products. Some commodities, however, such as cocoa, copper and cotton, have experienced significant earnings instability, and from this it follows that individual developing countries may well have had their development prospects affected by such instability. *Earnings instability may arise from either the demand side or the supply side.*

Demand fluctuations, beyond the control of the exporting countries, reflect changes in the level of economic activity in industrialized countries. A proportionate reduction in demand tending to have a greater adverse effect upon the total export earning from a commodity than an equivalent proportionate supply increase. Demand fluctuations have been large as in the world economic boom of 1972–74, the subsequent recession, and the impact of the Asian financial crisis on commodity prices.

If variations in *supply* are the major cause of export earnings instability, stabilizing prices will not stabilize earnings. Stable prices would reduce earnings in times of scarcity and increase them in times of glut. Much will depend on the *price elasticities* of demand and supply.

There are various types of **international commodity agreements.**

Buffer stock schemes

These operate by buying the commodity when the price falls below some agreed minimum level and selling the commodity when price rises above the agreed maximum level. Figure 10 represents a shift in demand. Price instability is caused by a shift in the demand line from D_1D_1 to D_2D_2. At D_3D_3, buffer stocks come into action. P_3 is the equilibrium price at which quantity demanded equals quantity supplied (both equal Q_3). If the actual price rises above P_3, say to P_2, then the buffer stock authorities will sell $Q_2 - Q_3$ in order to reduce price to P_3. If price falls to P_1, then the authorities buy $Q_3 - Q_1$ in order to raise price to P_3. In this case, price stabilization implies revenue stabilization.

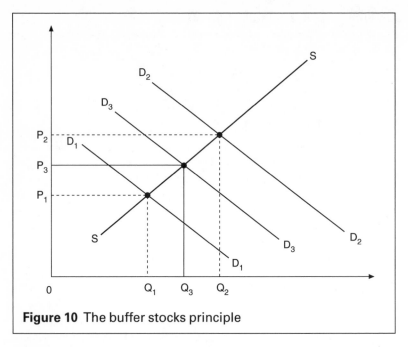

Figure 10 The buffer stocks principle

When the supply curve shifts the analysis becomes more complicated, because we then have to take into account the elasticity of demand. As a general rule, the more inelastic is the demand curve, the greater is the variation in price stabilization. Upper and lower price levels must be realistic and buffer stock authorities must have adequate resources to defend the lower price level. Often this is not the case and funds are exhausted defending unrealistic minimum prices. Both the International Cocoa Agreement in 1981 and the International Tin Agreement in 1985 collapsed for this reason.

Quota agreements

These schemes attempt to restrict supply in order to maintain the purchasing power of commodity exports in relation to industrial goods. Producer nations get together and agree to restrict production and exports by the allocation of a quota to each member of the agreement. There are often arguments over the allocation of quotas, and higher prices will tend to increase supply and create pressures for members to cheat. Consumers will also have an incentive to buy at lower prices either from non-member countries or illicitly from members. The International Coffee Agreement (now defunct) and OPEC are examples of such arrangements.

International compensatory finance

Rather than attempt to stabilize individual commodity prices, these schemes try to increase the level and stability of earnings from total exports.

The Lomé Convention, which is an agreement between the European Union (EU) and a number of African, Caribbean and Pacific (ACP) countries, has an export-earning stabilization scheme called STABEX. This applies to unexpected falls in export earnings of a selected number of products from ACP to the EU.

The IMF operates a more general compensatory financing facility which, since 1988, has been called the Compensatory and Contingency Financial Facility (CCFF). This covers fluctuations in foreign exchange earnings resulting from a variety of factors – changes in export and import prices, interest rate changes, tourist receipts and migrants' remittances, etc. – to encourage member countries to undertake long-term programmes.

Manufactured goods exports

Changes in the structure of output are reflected in changes in a country's exports, so as countries industrialize we would expect to see changes in the composition of exports, with a rise in the proportion of exported manufactures.

As noted already, by the end of the 1970s the value of manufactured goods exported by LDCs exceeded exports of food and raw materials and since then the rate of growth of manufactured exports has exceeded the rate of growth of raw materials exports.

But it is the economies of East and South East Asia that have dominated LDC exports of manufactured goods. As can be seen from Table 12, the top eight exporters of manufactured goods raised their share total world manufacturing exports from 1.5 per cent in 1963 to almost 20 per cent in 1995. As the two right-hand columns in Table 12 show, there have been striking changes in the composition of exports from many of these countries (not the change in Indonesia, Malaysia and Singapore, for example).

As noted in Chapter 4, global trade is still dominated by the developed market economies. Nevertheless, trade between developing countries (so-called 'South–South') trade is increasing in relative importance, especially among the countries of East Asia (excluding Japan).

There have been changes in the composition of manufactured goods exports. The share of processed products has risen, and some of the NIEs are becoming important exporters of more sophisticated commodities

Table 12 Growth of manufactured exports from newly industrializing countries, 1963–95

Country	Share of world total per cent		Average annual growth rate (%)		Manufacturers as % of total exports	
	1963	1995	1970/80	1980/94	1980	1994
East and South East Asia						
South Korea	0.01	3.1	22.7	12.3	89.4	92.7
Taiwan	0.20	2.9	16.5	10.0	88.0	93.7
Hong Kong	0.80	4.4	9.9	15.8	88.3	93.0
Singapore	0.40	2.7	–	12.7	43.0	82.1
Malaysia	0.10	1.5	3.3	12.6	18.7	83.6
Thailand	0.00	1.1	8.9	15.5	25.0	71.8
Indonesia	0.00	0.8	6.5	6.7	2.3	51.6
China	–	3.4	8.7	11.5	47.7	82.5
Subtotal	1.51	19.9				
Southern Asia						
India	0.80	0.6	5.9	7.0	51.4	75.6
Latin America						
Brazil	0.10	0.8	8.6	5.2	37.2	54.5
Argentina	–	–	8.9	3.2	23.1	33.7
Mexico	0.20	1.5	5.5	5.4	10.2	77.4
Southern Europe						
Spain	0.30	1.8	12.6	7.4	71.8	76.9
Portugal	0.30	0.4	1.5	10.6	70.3	72.2
Greece	–	–	11.7	5.3	46.5	50.6

Source: Dicken, 1998

embodying increasingly advanced technologies. Countries such as Singapore, Malaysia, Brazil, Indonesia, Morocco, the Philippines, Thailand, Tunisia and Turkey variously export chemical, medicinal and pharmaceutical products, electrical machinery and aircraft.

The more advanced NIEs, Taiwan and Korea in particular, faced with growing competition from lower-wage economies such as Indonesia and China, are moving to higher-valued production. This is in traditional areas, such as clothing, and in new priority sectors – computer peripherals, integrated circuits and automobiles. The

Koreans in particular have had great success in these areas, and have acquired the necessary technologies both through direct foreign investment (DFI – see Chapter 9) and by their own efforts in increased research and development expenditures.

Conclusions

International trade is inherently neither good nor bad. It creates new opportunities, incomes and jobs but it can also destroy them as technologies change and new centres of production emerge.

International trade has a higher profile today than perhaps at any other time in the recent past. The WTO has important implications for LDC trade, and **trade liberalization** is an important component of the majority of programmes for LDC economic reform and adjustment. On the other hand, international cooperation through commodity agreements aimed at stabilizing primary commodity prices is minimal, and many poor countries are faced with both unstable and declining prices for their major exports.

Those countries that have begun the process of industrialization and the export of manufactured goods have fared best in terms of economic growth. Smaller poorer countries still heavily dependent on the export of a limited range of primary commodities have few options and will remain dependent on the global community for their sustenance.

KEY WORDS

Open economies
Primary commodity exports
Comparative advantage
Uruguay Round
World Trade Organization
Net barter terms of trade

Instability
Price-takers
International commodity
   agreements
Trade liberalization

Further reading

Anderton, A., Unit 103 in *Economics*, 3rd edn, Causeway Press, 2000.
Hirst, P., and Thompson, G., Chapter 5 in *Globalization in Question*, 2nd edn, Polity Press, 1999.
Mackintosh *et al.*, Chapter 27 in *Economics and Changing Economies*, International Thomson Business Press, 1996.
Mankiw, N., Chapter 29 in *Principles of Economics*, Dryden Press, 1997.

Useful websites
UNICEF: www.unicef.org
World Trade Organization: www.into.org

Essay topics
1. (a) Examine the policies which could be adopted to increase the rate of economic growth in a country of your choice.   [60 marks]
   (b) How might a sharp fall in world commodity prices affect economic growth in the world economy?   [40 marks]
   [Edexcel, January 1999]
2. (a) Explain how a developing country's factor endowment influences where its comparative advantage lies.   [10 marks]
   (b) Discuss the policies the government of a developing country might introduce to improve its performance in international trade.
   [15 marks]

   [OCR specimen paper, 2000]

Data response question
This task is based on a question set by Edexcel in 1998. Read the article, which is adapted from 'Where investment outweighs trade in free markets' by D. Coyle, published in *The Independent* on 29 August 1996. Then answer the questions that follow.

International trade and investment
There used to be no ambiguity about it. From colonial times until about 10 years ago the links between the developed economies and the developing ones – 'North' and 'South' – consisted of a straightforward spillover. Good times in the North made for good times in the South too, and vice versa, so dependent were the poorer countries on exports to the richer ones. But times have changed. The newly industrializing countries have actually shed their dependence on the pace of growth in the industrial world. So concludes a new working paper from the International Monetary Fund. The link between Northern recession and slower Southern growth appears to have broken down in the late 1980s. Although this is too recent to draw firm conclusions, there seems to have been a structural change in the economies of the developing world, and mainly in South-East Asia. Northern growth has begun to depend on economic expansion in the South. The IMF paper puts forward three related explanations for the fact that Asia managed to buck the early 1990s recession in the industrialized world. These are (1) trade liberalization and other structural reforms introduced by the region's most

successful economies, (2) their increasingly diversified exports and (3) a huge increase in capital inflows.

It is the third, the increase in capital inflows, which is the most significant. Capital flows from North to South have risen dramatically since the late 1980s, with the increase in their value far outweighing the growth in the value of trade over the same period. Overseas investment by Northern companies has grown far faster than exports and imports. The Organization for Economic Co-operation and Development argues that it is the growth of investment rather than trade as the international means of doing business which characterizes "globalization". It goes on to point out that the notion of market access, fundamental to free trade and enshrined in international trade agreements, needs to change in scope. However, obstacles to foreign companies doing business on equal terms are widespread and often deeply embedded in the host country's culture.

The changing nature of international linkages sharpens the classic dilemmas posed by progress towards free trade. The theoretical case for free trade – that all countries can be made better off by trade – overlooks the likelihood that within countries there will be winners and losers. Those who are concerned about free trade have concerns over labour and environmental standards.

1. Using economic analysis, explain why economic growth in developing countries used to depend primarily on growth in the developed countries.   [6 marks]
2. Apart from capital flows, how might you explain that 'Asia managed to buck the early 1990s recession in the industrialized world'?   [6 marks]
3. How could private capital flows also help to explain the rapid growth in Asia?   [5 marks]
4. Discuss *two* concerns that foreign companies might have in contemplating investment in developing countries.   [4 marks]
5. Explain why, in any one country, free trade can give rise to 'winners and losers'.   [4 marks]

Chapter Nine

Transnational corporations and economic development

'Multinationals have changed their ideas about where their competitive advantage lies. They used to think that their most precious resource was capital, and that the prime task of management was to allocate it in the most productive way. Now they have become convinced that their most precious resource is knowledge, and that the prime task of management is to ensure that their knowledge is generated as widely and used as efficiently as possible.' The Economist, 24–30 June 1995

A transnational (or 'multinational') corporation (TNC) is an enterprise that owns *income-generating assets* such as mines, plantations, factories and sales offices in *different nation states*; that is, it engages in international production.

Unlike the national firm that exports all or part of its product, much of the trade of the TNC takes place within the corporation (**intra-corporate trade**) rather than between independent economic agents. Also, unlike the national firm that exports part of its factor inputs (material or human capital), the TNC, through **direct foreign investment** (DFI), supplies such inputs as a 'package' and maintains control of the use that is made of them.

It is estimated by the United Nations that by the end of the 1990s there were approximately 60 000 TNCs – that is **parent companies** – with between them approximately 500 000 **foreign affiliates** worldwide. Of that latter total, approximately 47 per cent were located in developing countries.

Table 13 illustrates the growing importance of TNCs originating in the semi-industrialized countries, such as Brazil, Korea and China.

The majority of TNCs are relatively small or medium-sized companies. The TNC population is, however, dominated by a relatively small number of very large TNCs which together held $1800 billion in foreign assets, sold products worth $2100 billion abroad and employed approximately six million people in their foreign affiliates in 1997 (UN, 1999). The top 100 TNCs accounted for an estimated 15 per cent of the foreign assets of all TNCs and 22 per cent of their sales.

These very large TNCs dominate a number of key sectors –

Table 13 The geographical distribution of parent transnational corporations and foreign affiliates in the 1990s (various years)

Region/economy	Parent corporations	Foreign affiliates*
Developed countries of which:	49 806	94 623
France	2 078	9 351
Germany	7 569	11 445
Japan	4 334	3 321
Switzerland	4 506	5 774
United Kingdom	1 085	2 525
USA	3 382	18 711
Developing countries of which:	9 246	238 906
Brazil	1,225	8 050
China	379	145 000
Hong Kong	500	5 312
India	187	1 416
Malaysia	–	3 787
Korea, Republic of	4 488	5 137
Taiwan	–	5 733
Singapore	–	18 154
Central and Eastern Europe	850	174 710
World totals	*59 902*	*508 239*

*Represents the number of foreign affiliates in the economy shown as defined by those countries. Note that these data vary significantly from preceding years.

Source: United Nations, *The World Investment Report,* 1992

petroleum, chemicals, pharmaceuticals, machinery and equipment, and motor vehicles. They include the best-known companies – General Motors, Ford, IBM, Toyota, General Electric, Unilever – as well as the petroleum giants. Table 14 shows the 'Top Twenty'.

Direct foreign investment
TNCs enter new markets largely through direct foreign investment, often using **joint-venture** arrangements in which they are either majority or minority **equity** holders. **Non-equity operations** include **licensing** and **franchising**, where the TNC is not an equity holder but where it can exercise control through, for example, the supply of technology or management.

Table 14 The world's top 20 TNCs, ranked by foreign assets, 1997 (billions of dollars and number of employees)

Ranking by foreign assets		
Corporation	Country	Industry
1 General Electric	US	Electronics
2 Ford Motor Company	US	Automotive
3 Royal Dutch/Shell Group	Netherlands/UK	Petroleum expl./ref./distr.
4 General Motors	US	Automotive
5 Exxon Corporation	US	Petroleum expl./ref./distr.
6 Toyota	Japan	Automotive
7 IBM	US	Computers
8 Volkswagen Group	Germany	Automotive
9 Nestlé SA	Switzerland	Food and beverages
10 Daimler-Benz AG	Germany	Automotive
11 Mobil Corporation	US	Petroleum expl./ref./distr
12 FIAT Spa	Italy	Automotive
13 Hoechst AG	Germany	Chemicals
14 Asea Brown Boveri (ABB)	Switzerland	Electrical equipment
15 Bayer AG	Germany	Chemicals
16 Elf Aquitaine SA	France	Petroleum expl./ref./distr
17 Nissan Motor Co. Ltd	Japan	Automotive
18 Unilever	Netherlands/UK	Food and beverages
19 Siemens AG	Germany	Electronics
20 Roche Holding AG	Switzerland	Pharmaceuticals

Source: UNCTAD/Erasmus University database

In the 1990s, TNCs had increasingly been operating through non-equity arrangements, including strategic partnerships, especially in the information technology, pharmaceutical and automobile industries. Knowledge-based networks, not captured in traditional measures of international production, were a crucial factor of market power in some industries (UN, 1999). Cross-border mergers and acquisitions (M&As), for example the takeover of Amoco by BP for $55 billion and the acquisition of Chrysler by Daimler-Benz for $44.5 billion, drove the growth of DFI flows between the developed market economies in the late-1990s.

The global inward stock of DFI in 1998 was estimated by the UN at $4100 billion, up from $3400 billion in 1997. Inflows of DFI were $644 billion in 1998 as compared with $464 billion in 1997 (UN, 1999). Virtually all of this increase was concentrated in the developed economies. For developing countries, inward DFI flows decreased from $173 billion in 1997 to £166 billion in 1998. The 48 least developed countries attracted less than £3 billion, accounting for 1.8 per cent of flows to all developing countries and 0.5 per cent of global DFI flows.

Table 15 presents data on DFI inflows in 1998 by host region and major recipient economies. Over the period 1987–92, the developed economies accounted for approximately 78 per cent of DFI inflows and the less-developed economies accounted for 20 per cent. By 1998 the share of the developed economies had fallen to 71.5 per cent and that of the LDCs had risen to 25.7 per cent. In 1997, however, the LDCs share had been 37 per cent, largely accounted for by increased inflows into Asia in that year. Note that the Asian financial crisis of 1997 led to

Table 15 ADFI Inflows by host region and economy, 1987–98 (millions of dollars)

World	1987 – 92 annual average	1998
	173 530	643 879
Developed countries	136 628	460 431
of which:		
USA	46 211	193 375
Developing countries	35 326	165 936
Africa		
(incl. South Africa)	3 010	7 931
		(8 302)
Latin America and the Caribbean	12 400	71 652
of which:		
Brazil	1 513	28 718
Asia	19 613	84 880
of which:		
China	4 652	45 460
The Pacific	220	175
Central and eastern Europe	1 576	17 513
of which:		
Poland	183	5 129

Source: UNCTAD, *World Investment Report 1999*

significant falls in DFI inflows in a number of important countries (especially China, Indonesia, Malaysia and Taiwan Province of China). Thailand and Korea saw major increases in DFI inflows in 1998 and in the case of Korea a further significant increase to US$15.5 billion in 1999.

Table 16 gives details of the 'Top Ten' developing-economy recipients of DFI in 1998. Note that these economies accounted for approximately 73 per cent of total developing inflows in that year.

Why do LDCs want DFI?

Despite the reservations that many LDCs have had in the past concerning the role of foreign capital in the development process, competition between LDCs for TNC investment is probably greater now than ever before. This competition has been intensified by the changes that have occurred in eastern and central Europe and the former Soviet Union and by the emergence of China as a capital importer.

TNCs own, control or have access to vast resources of capital, technology and all kinds of expertise – financial, managerial, marketing – and often provide access to export markets. These are the factors that are absent or in short supply in LDCs, and the main attraction of TNC investment is that these resources are all part of the DFI 'package'. The TNC appears to be the 'engine of growth' that can solve the problems of underdevelopment and poverty.

Many radical economists would argue that precisely the opposite is the case; the TNCs exploit LDCs through the extraction of raw materials for which they do not pay a fair price, through their use of

Table 16 'Top Ten' developing country recipients of DFI in 1998 (millions of dollars)

China	45 460
Brazil	28 718
Mexico	10 238
Singapore	7 218
Thailand	6 969
Argentina	5 697
Rep. of Korea	5 143
Chile	4 792
Venezuela	3 737
Malaysia	3 727
Total	121 699

Source : UNCTAD, 1999

WHY DO TNCs INVEST IN LDCs?

In order to invest overseas, an enterprise must possess an advantage or asset not shared by its local competitors. In addition, it is the use of those assets or advantages within the enterprise – their **internalization** – that gives the TNC its unique advantages.

The competitive strengths of TNCs are obvious from what has already been said. Clearly TNCs have a preference for investing in already developed economies and the middle- or upper-income poorer economies. So what motivates TNC investments in poor countries? The following factors are of importance:

- the exploitation of raw materials either not found in other countries or more cheaply available in poor countries – iron ore, bauxite, copper;
- the exploitation of the agricultural potential of the poor country via large-scale agribusiness – ranching, soya beans, pineapples, sugar;
- the exploitation of large and/or rapidly growing domestic markets via ISI (see Chapter 8) – cigarettes, soft drinks, automobiles, cosmetics – where it is important that TNCs establish themselves to safeguard their markets from competitors;
- the use of low-wage, non-unionized, often predominantly female labour in export processing zones (EPZs) in assembly or processing activities – electronics, garments.

Different types of DFI are influenced by differing economic factors. All TNCs, however, require political stability in host economies, with freedom from arbitrary expropriation and with the guarantee of profit repatriation.

---

cheap labour, and through the transfer of 'inappropriate' technology and products. There are also well-documented cases of TNCs interfering in political affairs and destabilizing governments.

Opinion has changed over the past 15 years, however. There is now wider agreement that TNCs can make an important contribution to development, although governments must create the conditions to ensure that the full potential of DFI for development is realized.

TNCs and development

Technology transfer and employment

It is generally agreed that TNCs are the major channel for the transfer of new technologies in less-developed countries. But are those technologies 'appropriate' with respect to the resource endowments and development objectives of LDCs?

OECD imposes ethical code on multinationals

CHARLOTTE DENNY

Western governments yesterday agreed an international code of conduct for multinational companies which they hailed as a breakthrough in holding corporations to account for abuses of workers and the environment throughout the world.

After a tense two days of negotiations. during which Mexico demanded of the other 28 members of the Organisation for Economic Cooperation and Development that standards be watered down, an agreement was hammered out early yesterday.

The guidelines replace an earlier OECD code and for the first time incorporate human rights and core labour standards. However, they are still voluntary and there are no procedures for imposing sanctions on offending companies.

The Guardian, 28 June 2000

Critics of TNCs argue that the technologies they transfer are largely capital-intensive – that is, they require the use of a large amount of capital per unit of labour employed. *As a consequence, DFI creates few new jobs and prevents the use and development of more labour-intensive technologies which might be more consistent with LDC employment-creation objectives.* Whether or not TNCs can or will develop new technologies specifically suited to the economic conditions found in poorer countries remains an open question.

The impact of DFI on the balance of payments
Credit items in the balance of payments (BoP) will include:

- the initial act of DFI which usually brings new capital into the host economy (although sometimes TNCs will borrow from local banks or other sources with no new capital transferred);
- exports that result from the DFI;
- a reduction in imports if the DFI is import-substituting (but see Chapter 7).

Debit items in the BoP will include:

- imports of machinery and equipment, raw materials and intermediate goods not available locally;

- payments made by the subsidiary to the parent company for technical and managerial inputs – royalties and other fees;
- the repatriation of profits made by the subsidiary back to the parent or some other part of the TNC.

Whether the net balance-of-payments effect of DFI is positive or negative is an empirical issue that can be settled only by looking at the data for a specific country over a given period. But this is more complicated than it seems because TNCs use *intra-corporate* or **transfer prices** on all transactions that take place within the enterprise. Such prices can differ from market prices, and TNCs will set transfer prices to meet their global corporate objectives in profit-maximization, tax-minimization, the minimization of risks, etc.

Conclusions

There always exists the potential for clashes of interest between transnational corporations and host governments. TNCs are concerned with their global objectives whereas national governments are concerned with national development objectives. It has been suggested above that conflicts might well arise with respect to technology, employment and the balance of payments.

Clearly TNCs have a broader impact on the countries they invest in. They introduce new products with their marketing and advertising techniques and create new 'lifestyles'. They may well displace traditional products and eliminate local competition, destroying old jobs as well as creating new jobs.

However, if it is the case that – as a quote from *The Economist* at the start of this chapter argues – the real power of the TNCs lies in their ownership of *knowledge*, then for the LDC the real value of direct foreign investment is the potential knowledge that it makes available to the host economy. The problem for the LDC government is to create the framework within which that knowledge is most efficiently and effectively acquired.

KEY WORDS

Intra-corporate trade	Non-equity operations
Direct foreign investment	Licensing
Parent companies	Franchising
Foreign affiliates	Internalization
Joint ventures	Transfer prices
Equity	Transfer prices

Further reading

Atkinson, B., Livesey, F., and Milward, R., Chapter 7 in *Applied Economics*, Macmillan, 1998.

Davies, B., Hale, G., Smith, C., and Tiller, H., Chapter 5.33 in *Investigating Economics*, Macmillan, 1996.

Griffiths, A., and Wall, S. (eds) , Chapter 7 in *Applied Economics*, 8th edn, Longman, 1999.

Sloman, J., Chapter 26 in *Economics*, 4th edn, Prentice Hall, 1999.

Useful websites

Bized gateway to selected company reports: www.bized.ac.uk/dataserv/comrep.htm

World Economic Outlook Database (IMF): www.imf.org/external

Essay topics

1. (a) Explain the relevance to developing countries of: (i) using the appropriate technology, and (ii) globalization.   [8 marks]
    (b) Discuss the contribution made by multinational corporations to the process of development.   [12 marks]
    [OCR, June 2000]
2. (a) Explain why domestically generated investment is often low in developing countries.   [10 marks]
    (b) Discuss why some multinationals invest in developing countries.   [10 marks]

Data response question

This task is based on a question set by Edexcel in 1999. Read the article, which is from *The Economist* of 22 November 1997. Then answer the questions that follow.

Multinationals

'Multinational corporations stand at the heart of the debate over the merits of global economic integration. Their critics portray them as bullies, using their power to exploit workers and natural resources with no regard for the economic well-being of any country or community. Their supporters see multinationals as a triumph for global capitalism.

Both of these stereotypes have some truth to them. But it would be wrong to portray the multinational corporation as either good or evil. Companies become multinational in many different ways and for many different reasons. Their impact on the global economy is far from simple to determine.

Today, as for many years, roughly three-fifths of all foreign direct investment goes into wealthy countries and two-fifths into "developing" countries. Those two-fifths, however, are not flowing into the same countries; China, now the leading recipient of foreign investment among developing countries, received almost none in the 1980s. Africa, despite its rich natural resources, receives almost no foreign direct investment.

Multinationals' size and scale can make it possible for them to exert power in an exploitative way. Another common criticism is that multinationals are exporting jobs to low-wage countries. This may be true in some industries, such as textiles and electronics, but in most cases it is exaggerated.'

1. Explain the meaning of the statement that 'their supporters see multinationals as a triumph for global capitalism'. [3 marks]
2. With reference to the passage, examine the factors which might explain why some countries attract more foreign investment than others. [8 marks]
3. The passage refers to multinationals 'exporting jobs'. Discuss the impact on employment in *developed* countries of multinationals investing in developed countries. [6 marks]
4. Apart from labour cost considerations, identify what other benefits a multinational company might enjoy from having interests in several countries. [4 marks]
5. To what extent is official development finance an effective substitute for private capital flows for countries unable to attract investment by multinationals? [4 marks]

Chapter Ten

Aid and debt

'The goal must be to make aid a more effective weapon in the war against global poverty. This entails challenges for donors and recipients alike.' World Bank, 1990

What is foreign aid?

Foreign aid consists of transfers of real resources to LDCs on **concessional terms**. It excludes purely commercial transactions and should exclude military aid which does not have as its objective the promotion of economic development.

Aid can be given in various forms:

- as grants or loans;
- as technical assistance;
- as commodity (largely food) aid.

There may be various forms of **conditionality** attached. For example, aid may be given for a *project* (to build a road) or made available for a *programme* (to improve the transport sector).

Bilateral aid is given by the aid agency of one country (e.g. the UK Department for International Development, DFID) to recipients in another.

Multilateral aid (through the EU, the World Bank or a UN agency) is usually considered superior to bilateral aid as it avoids the problems that might arise in bilateral one-to-one relationships.

Bilateral aid is normally **tied** to a particular project or programme and must be spent in the donor country. Multilateral aid may be tied to a specific project or programme but cannot require that the funds are spent in a particular country.

Aid refers only to economic assistance that qualifies as 'official development assistance' (ODA), which is grants or loans:

- undertaken by the official sector;
- with the promotion of economic development as its main objectives;
- at concessional financial terms – this involves calculation of the **grant element** of a loan (the difference between market interest rates and repayment terms and those actually charged on the loan) which must be at least 25 per cent for a loan to qualify as ODA.

Table 17 Total net resource flows from DAC member countries and multilateral agencies to aid recipients (current billions of dollars)

Official Development Finance (ODF)	1991	1992	1993	1994	1995	1996	1997	1998*
	84.5	78.3	82.4	84.5	87.6	73.5	75.3	88.3
(A) Official development assistance (ODA) †	57.1	58.3	55.5	59.6	59.1	55.8	47.7	49.7
of which:								
Bilateral	41.4	41.4	39.4	41.3	40.6	39.1	32.4	35.1
Multilateral	15.8	17.0	16.1	18.3	18.4	16.7	15.3	14.5
(B) Total Export Credits	0.6	1.0	–3.0	6.3	5.6	4.0	4.8	4.0
(C) Private flows	53.0	80.1	86.3	134.7	176.0	291.7	244.9	147.2
Direct investment (DAC)	24.8	30.2	41.6	52.1	59.6	69.7	106.7	118.0
International bank lending ‡	10.7	34.6	4.8	32.1	76.9	86.0	12.0	–65.0
Total bond lending	4.9	7.5	28.7	32.0	30.0	96.6	83.2	39.8
Other (including equities)	7.1	1.8	5.5	12.5	3.5	33.8	37.8	49.1
Grants by non-governmental organizations	5.4	6.0	5.7	6.0	6.0	5.6	5.2	5.4
Total net resource flows (A+B+C)	138.1	159.4	165.7	285.5	269.1	369.2	324.9	239.6
Memorandum items (not included):								
Interest paid by aid recipients	–75.9	–68.0	–64.6	–83.2	–105.0	–103.2	–114.0	–112.2
Net use of IMF credit **	3.6	0.8	3.3	0.6	15.6	0.3	14.4	18.8

* Provisional.

† excluding forgiveness of non-ODA debt for the years 1991 to 1992.

‡ Excluding bond lending by banks (item III.3.), and guaranteed financial credits (included in II).

§ Incomplete reporting from several DAC countries (including France, the United Kingdom and the United States). Includes Japan from 1996.

** Non-concessional flows from the IMF General Resources Account.

Source: OECD, *Development Co-operation Report,* 1999

Table 17 gives details of total net resource flows to developing countries. The highlights are:

- fluctuations in levels of **official development finance** (ODF) in current prices, with marked falls between 1991 and 1992 and 1995 and 1996 (ODF includes official flows for development purposes but which have too low a grant element to qualify as aid);
- a fall in ODA in current prices over the period 1991 to 1998, with a small increase between 1997 and 1998;

- a significant fall in the shares in total net resource flows of both ODF and ODA;
- a major increase in flows of direct foreign investment (DFI) to less developed countries, with an especially large increase between 1996 and 1997 (note that DFI flows in aggregate do not appear to have been affected by the 1997 East Asian financial crisis);
- a significant increase in international bank lending overall, with a large fall between 1994 and 1996; the 1997 Asian financial crisis led to the collapse of these inflows in 1997 with massive outflows in 1998; bond lending follows a similar, although less dramatic pattern between 1997 and 1998.

Table 18 shows changes in the composition of net resource flows. In the 1970s there was a shift towards private flows which was given added weight by the aid policies of the Reagan and Thatcher administrations. The Mexican debt crisis of 1982 and its generalization to the rest of the Third World led to a fall in private flows and an increase in the relative importance of ODF and ODA. There were further changes between 1990 and 1993, with private flows once again accounting for more than 50 per cent of total resource flows. International bank lending, however, fluctuated between 1990 and 1993, with a peak in 1992 followed by a low in 1993.

Table 18 Total net resource flows to developing countries (percentage of total)

	1970	1980	1985	1990	1993	1994	1998
Official development finance (ODF) of which:	44.7	29.6	56.4	54.9	40.9	37.5	36.9
Official development assistance (ODA)	39.7	23.6	42.1	41.5	33.0	26.4	20.7
Total export credits	13.6	13.9	5.1	3.4	3.0	2.8	1.7
Private flows of which:	41.7	56.5	38.5	41.8	56.1	59.7	61.5
International bank lending	15.0	42.3	19.4	21.3	5.3	14.2	–27.1

Note: The figures for 1994 and 1998 are not strictly comparable with the earlier figures. These data are being continuously revised and later revisions do not always match earlier, often incomplete, data.

Source: OECD, *Development Co-operation*, various years

At the end of 1994, Mexico suffered another crisis. Political instability and economic uncertainty triggered a massive outflow of capital, a fall in stock market prices and a devaluation of the peso. 1995 witnessed efforts by the USA and the IMF to provide a financial rescue package.

As already noted, there was a massive increase in private flows up to 1997 with the IMF and other multilateral and bilateral institutions providing massive resource packages to the most affected Asian economies (mainly Indonesia, Thailand and the Republic of Korea).

Main features of the UK's aid programme

It was announced in July 2000 that there was to be an average 6.2 per cent increase (in real terms) in DIFD's expenditure over the next three years, taking it to almost £3.6 billion by year 2003/4. The UK government is committed to raising the share of aid in GNP from 0.29 per cent in 2000/1 to 0.33 per cent in 2003/4 (see Table 19).

Table 19 Major recipients of UK aid (gross disbursements; per cent of total ODA)

1977–78		1987–88		1997–98	
India	13.3	India	6.0	India	4.8
Bangladesh	4.4	Bangladesh	2.7	Guyana	3.1
Pakistan	2.9	Kenya	2.7	Tanzania	2.9
Kenya	2.6	Tanzania	2.1	Zambia	2.4
Zambia	1.6	Malawi	2.0	Uganda	2.4
Malawi	1.6	Mozambique	1.9	Bangladesh	2.2
Jamaica	1.4	Ghana	1.8	Mozambique	1.7
Solomon Islands	1.2	Sudan	1.6	Ghana	1.6
Tanzania	1.1	Pakistan	1.6	Montserrat	1.4
Swaziland	1.0	Zambia	1.5	China	1.3
Vanuatu	0.8	Uganda	1.3	Kenya	1.3
Sri Lanka	0.8	Sri Lanka	1.1	Indonesia	1.3
Sudan	0.8	Ethopia	1.0	South Africa	1.2
Indonesia	0.8	Zimbabwe	1.0	Pakistan	1.2
Nigeria	0.8	China	1.0	Malawi	1.1
Total above	35.2	*Total above*	29.3	*Total above*	29.9

Source: OECD, *Development Co-operation*, 1999

In the period 1979–83 the average was 0.40 per cent, and the UN 'target' is 0.70 per cent. Only four donor countries (Denmark, Norway, Sweden and the Netherlands) ever meet or exceed that target.

The aid relationship

Many economic and political issues arise in the aid relationship:

- why donors give aid;
- why poor countries accept aid;
- how aid should be given:
  - loans versus grants
  - tied versus untied aid
  - bilateral versus multilateral aid
  - project versus programme aid;
- which countries should be given aid;
- the impact of aid on the process of growth and development.

Even after 50 years' experience of aid, clear and simple answers cannot be given to these issues. Aid by itself cannot solve problems of poverty and inequality, but most people accept that aid should be made available to the poorest and most vulnerable in order to help alleviate their plight.

More recent work by the World Bank (1998) seems to suggest the following:

- Financial aid works in a good policy environment (sound economic management).
- Improvements in the economic institutions and policies in the LDCs are the key to the alleviation of poverty and foreign aid can provide critical support to such improvements.
- Effective aid complements private investment (with sound economic management, foreign aid 'crowds in' private investment; the opposite is the case with poor economic management.
- The value of development profits is to strengthen institutions and policies in order to ensure more effective service delivery.
- An active civil society improves public services – the best aid projects change the way that the public sector does business.
- Aid can promote reform in even the most adverse conditions but it requires patience and a focus on ideas, not money.

Not everyone would agree with these conclusions, and the debate on aid will not be resolved in the near future.

Third World debt

The global **debt crisis** erupted in 1982 when Mexico came close to defaulting on its international obligations. In 1970, total LDC external debt had stood at $68 billion. It had risen to $635.8 billion in 1980 and in 1982 it stood at $846.6 billion. After a brief spell when it grew only slowly, growth again accelerated and the total stood at $1421 billion in 1990 and $1630 billion in 1993. In 1996, the total stood at over $2000 billion. The largest LDC debtors, in terms of total debt, are listed in Table 20.

However, the absolute size of a country's debt is less important than its ability to service that debt – that is, to make interest and capital repayments. There are various ways of measuring the debt burden and different measures will produce differing rankings of indebtedness. Only three of the top ten debtors in absolute terms have the highest **debt service ratios** (debt service as a percentage of exports of goods and services); they are Agentina, Brazil and Mexico. Only Sâo Tome and Principe appears in both the top ten ranked by debt service ratio and ranked by debt as a percentage of GNP (see Table 21). Six of the latter ten countries appear in the Heavily Indebted Poor Countries (HIPC) list. It should also be noted that these ratios change radically from year to year, owing to changes in rates of growth of GNP and exports.

The acquisition of debt does not necessarily lead to debt problems. Borrowing increases the resources that countries have access to, and

Table 20 Top ten debtor countries, 1997 (absolute amount in $US billions, and as percentage of GNP)

	US$ billions	GNP (%)
Brazil	193.7	24.1
Mexico	149.7	38.4
China	146.7	16.6
Rep. of Korea	143.4	32.8
Indonesia	136.2	65.3
Russian Federation	125.6	28.7
Argentina	123.2	38.7
India	94.4	24.9
Thailand	93.4	62.6
Turkey	91.2	47.1

Source: UNDP, 1999

Table 21 Top ten debtor countries, 1997 (debt as percentage of GNP)

	%
São Tome & Principe	671.2
Nicaragua	305.6
Congo	278.4
Guyana	236.0
Bahrain	138.4
Syrian Arabic Republic	126.4
Jordan	121.0
Cameroon	109.2
Honduras	102.8
Bulgaria	101.3

Source: UNDP, 1999

provided that those resources are used in a productive manner – that is, generate an *income* that permits the debt to be serviced – then a debt problem should not emerge. If the debt has to be repaid in a foreign currency, then clearly the resources borrowed must, directly or indirectly, generate the foreign exchange needed for repayment. In other words, debtor countries have to run a balance-of-payments current account surplus in order to repay their debts.

Debt problems arise for a variety of reasons. Interest rates may rise and export prices fall. ODA may be reduced. Natural disasters or political instability ususally lead to falls in output. Sometimes commercial banks over-lend for the wrong reasons to the wrong countries/institutions/people. Poor countries may misuse the resources that incurring debt makes available. The flight of capital from poorer to richer countries has also been a major problem. Debt crisis is thus a complex problem. The type of debt varies between countries, as do the benefits that debtor countries have derived from the various international debt alleviation schemes.

Highly Indebted Poor Countries

In 1996, a proposal was put forward by the IMF and World Bank to alleviate the debt burden of the HIPCs in a comprehensive way. Almost the entire debt of the HIPCs is owed to official creditors, both bilateral and multilateral, and the objective of the **HIPC** Initiative was to cancel or reduce debt in order to make debt repayment sustainable. Debtor countries were required to demonstrate good policy performance within the context of the IMF/World Bank structural adjustment programmes. The HIPC was judged to be less than completely successful because of the small number potentially benefiting from it. Programmes were not targeted at poverty alleviation and countries found it difficult to meet IMF/World Bank conditionality.

In June 1999 in Cologne, the attempt was made to tie **debt relief** to poverty alleviation. The criteria for defining HIPCs were broadened and more countries were likely to benefit from more relief. Further commitments to debt relief were made in September 1999 at the annual meeting of the IMF/World Bank and at the G-8 summit in July 2000. Critics argue that only $10.6 billion of debt has so far been actually cancelled, as against the target set by Jubilee 2000, a coalition of development charities and non-governmental organizations working on the problem of debt relief.

Conclusions

The aid relationship is a complex one. Aid is not always given for the right reasons to the right people. It is part of a broader political strategic picture in which the promotion of development might be secondary, so there is no clear link between aid and development. But this is *not* an argument against aid as such. Donors can improve the quality of the aid they give and recipients can ensure that the projects and sectors receiving aid are consistent with national development activities. As the World Bank argues, both sides have responsibility if aid is to become a more effective weapon in the war against poverty.

KEY WORDS

Concessional terms	Grant element
Conditionality	Official development finance
Bilateral aid	Debt crisis
Multilateral aid	Debt service ratioss
Tied aid	HIPC
Official development assistance (ODA)	Debt relief

Further reading

Anderton, A., Unit 104 in *Economics*, 3rd edn, Causeway Press, 2000.

Bamford, C., and Grant, S., Chapter 8 in *The UK Economy in a Global Context*, Heinemann Educational, 2000.

Grant, S., Chapter 65 in *Stanlake's Introductory Economics*, 7th edn, Longman, 2000.

Sloman, J., Chapter 26 in *Economics*, 4th edn, Prentice Hall, 1999.

Useful websites

Jubilee 2000: www.jubilee2000uk.org
OECD: www.oecd.org

Essay topics

1. (a) Explain the circumstances which might justify a developing economy being granted foreign aid. [8 marks]
   (b) Discuss the case for making food aid the main form of foreign aid. [12 marks]
   [OCR, June 2000]
2. (a) Describe the main forms that foreign aid can take. [6 marks]
   (b) Discuss the view that for developing countries foreign aid can cause more problems than it solves. [14 marks]
   [UCLES, June 1998]

Data response question

This task is based on a question set by OCR in a specimen paper in 2000. Read the article and study the data in Figure A. Then answer the questions that follow.

African debt repayments 'imperial 21m children'

The cost of debt repayments by the world's poorest countries is overwhelming their efforts to save children's lives and provide a basic education, according to a report issued today by Oxfam.

Governments in sub-Saharan Africa transfer to creditors four times as much as they spend on healthcare, and more than they spend on primary education plus primary healthcare.

Zambia dramatically illustrates the trend. Per capita spending on primary school children is one-sixth of the level of a decade ago, and health spending is 30 per cent lower. On the most optimistic budget projections, Zambia will have spent $26 million on primary education in 1995. Its obligations to multilateral creditors are around $127 million.

There are 32 countries classified by the World Bank as severely indebted low-income countries (SILICs). They have debt-service-to-gross-national-product ratios of more than 80 per cent, or debt-service-to-export ratios of over 220 per cent.

Last year repayments of $16 billion fell due, but they were able to pay less than half this amount, with the rest added to arrears. For some countries the gap between their obligations and ability to pay has grown well beyond what could ever be paid back.

In recent years, these countries have been able to reschedule their debt, although this is only a temporary solution. The IMF plays a role here by advocating long-term structural change to the economy which makes rescheduling more likely by encouraging confidence in the economy. This approach usually involves programmes of devaluation, deflation and more use of the market system.

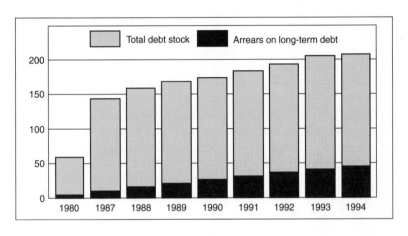

Figure A US public debt and arrears for 32 SILIC (US$ billions)

1. (a) With reference to Figure A, what happened to the debt position of severely indebted low-income countries between 1980 and 1994? [2 marks]

   (b) Show, with an example from the article, how opportunity cost applies to debt repayment. [2 marks]

2. (a) What is meant by a 'debt-service-to-export ratio' and why is a figure of over 220 per cent significant? [2 marks]

   (b) Explain *two* possible reasons for increases in debt ratios of developing economies. [4 marks]

3. (a) State *one* way in which debt can be rescheduled. [1 mark]

   (b) Explain the operation of any *one* of the structural adjustment policies favoured by the IMF. [3 marks]

4. Discuss how the debt position of sub-Saharan African countries might affect their prospects of development. [6 marks]

Conclusion

This book has attempted to identify and discuss a number of the issues and problems currently faced by developing countries.

Economic development has been pursued by poor countries in an attempt to raise *per capita* incomes and to change the structures of production and trade largely inherited from the colonial period.

Some countries have succeeded in this task and valuable insights can be drawn from their experiences. Other countries have been less successful, and massive problems remain with regard to poverty, inequality, unemployment and, increasingly, environmental degradation. There is no single model of development, however, and country-specific strategies and policies cannot be simplistically transferred to other countries with different histories, structures, institutions and cultures. In part because of the perceived failure of development in so many countries, pro-poor growth strategies and a more explicit commitment to poverty alleviation are now high on the development agenda.

Chapters 1 and 2 discussed a variety of related issues – the nature and dimensions of poverty, the meaning and measurement of development and problems of terminology. It is argued that development is a normative concept that incorporates our value judgements. This makes it difficult to define and problems of measurement remain.

Chapter 3 considered the theoretical origins of development economics and alternative theoretical approaches to the analysis of development and the prescribing of policies. All economic theories have to abstract from reality and make general statements. Even though economists have produced original theories, incorporating both the specific and general characteristics of developing countries, there remain arguments between neoclassical and structuralist schools of thought. It is unlikely that such debates will ever be resolved.

Chapter 4 emphasized the vulnerability of developing countries to external 'shocks' beyond their direct control. Some of the relevant issues were discussed in Chapters 7 to 10. The openness of their economies, in terms of the importance of international trade and international capital movements, the dependence of many poor countries on a limited range of commodity exports and markets, and problems of external indebtedness, all influence the process of growth and development. Transnational corporations ('multinationals') provide technology and expertise in various forms, but there is always the possibility of a clash of interests with host country governments which may not be resolved in the latter's favour. Globalization, too, provides new opportunities to poor countries; but it also poses new problems and it is not yet clear how well poor countries will be able to deal with those.

One of the main arguments presented in the book is that industrialization is a necessary, but not sufficient, condition for high and sustained rates of growth of *per capita* income and structural transformation. Modernization of the agricultural sector is of strategic importance in this respect.

The emergence of the NICs presents an example of successful industrialization. There are conflicting explanations as to why some East and South East Asian economies have been so successful, with debate focusing on the balance between the market on the one hand and state intervention on the other. The extent to which developing countries can emulate the success of the NICs remains an open question.

The 1997 financial crisis had led to significant changes in a number of affected economies, especially Korea. It is by no means certain that the post-1997 'model' of Korean development will resemble the very successful pre-1997 strategy.

Chapter 6 considered issues of population and the environment. Some environmental problems are the consequence of the lack of economic development; others are problems of 'success' – congestion on the roads of capital cities, for example. Environmental issues now have a profile in the development debate which is higher than ever before. To what extent such concerns will be incorporated effectively into the policymaking process is still unclear, however. Environmental and macroeconomic policies may remain in conflict with one another.

Countries that are collectively defined as the Third World exhibit greater disparities in experience and economic performance. Gaps between rich and poor countries are being made more complex by increasing inequalities between the more-developed, less-developed and least-developed developing countries. Within individual countries, there are huge inequalities in the distribution of income and wealth (see Chapter 5), with profound repercussions on the development process. The notion that there are large numbers of very rich people in very poor countries is an unsettling one!

The majority of social scientists who study the development of poor countries accept that it is a complex, multidimensional process. Historical, institutional, social and political factors all need to be taken into account in order that we are able to reach a better understanding of the processes of growth and development.

Index